This series offers the concerned reader basic guidelines and *practical* applications of religion for today's world. Although decidedly Christian in focus and emphasis, the series embraces all denominations and modes of Bible-based belief relevant to our lives today. All volumes in the Steeple series are originals, freshly written to provide a fresh perspective on current—and yet timeless—human dilemmas. This is a series for our times.

Walking in the Garden:
Inner Peace from the Flowers of God
Paula Connor

How to Bring up Children in the Catholic Faith
Carol and David Powell

Sex in the Bible: An Introduction to What the Scriptures
Teach Us About Sexuality
Michael R. Cosby

How to Talk with God Every Day of the Year:
A Book of Devotions for Twelve Positive Months
Frances Hunter

God's Conditions for Prosperity:
How to Earn the Rewards of Christian Living
Charles Hunter

Pilgrimages: A Guide to the Holy Places
of Europe for Today's Traveler
Paul Lambourne Higgins

Journey into the Light: Lessons of Pain and Joy
to Renew Your Energy and Strengthen Your Faith
Dorris Blough Murdock

Paula Connor works at a private school for emotionally disturbed children. An avid nature lover, she is a former Sunday school teacher.

PRENTICE-HALL INTERNATIONAL, INC., *London*
PRENTICE-HALL OF AUSTRALIA PTY. LIMITED, *Sydney*
PRENTICE-HALL OF CANADA, INC., *Toronto*
PRENTICE-HALL OF INDIA PRIVATE LIMITED, *New Delhi*
PRENTICE-HALL OF JAPAN, INC., *Tokyo*
PRENTICE-HALL OF SOUTHEAST ASIA PTE. LTD., *Singapore*
WHITEHALL BOOKS LIMITED, *Wellington, New Zealand*
EDITORA PRENTICE-HALL DO BRASIL LTD., *Rio de Janeiro*

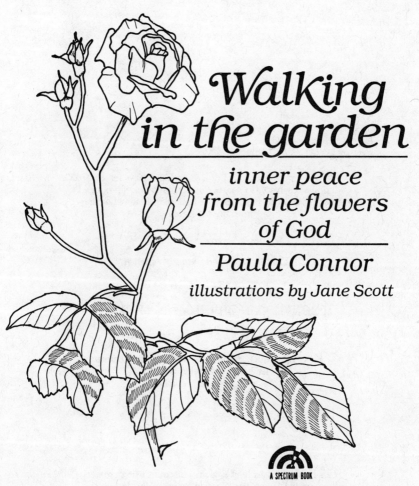

Walking in the garden

inner peace from the flowers of God

Paula Connor

illustrations by Jane Scott

A SPECTRUM BOOK

Prentice-Hall, Inc.
Englewood Cliffs, New Jersey 07632

Library of Congress Cataloging in Publication Data

Connor, Paula.
    Walking in the garden.

    A Spectrum Book.
    (Steeple books)
    Includes bibliographical references.
    1. Meditations. I. Title. II. Series.
BV4832.2.C635   1984   242   83-13967
ISBN 0-13-944280-4
ISBN 0-13-944264-2 (pbk.)

A SPECTRUM BOOK

Printed in the United States of America

1 2 3 4 5 6 7 8 9 10

ISBN 0-13-944264-2 {PBK.}

ISBN 0-13-944280-4

Editorial/production supervision by Claudia Citarella
Cover design by Hal Siegel
Manufacturing buyer: Ed Ellis

This book is available at a special discount when ordered
in bulk quantities. Contact Prentice-Hall, Inc.,
General Publishing Division, Special Sales,
Englewood Cliffs, New Jersey 07632.

To my sons, Daniel and David, and my mother, Pauline

O Lord, I will praise you
with all my heart, and tell
everyone about the marvelous
things you do.

Psalm 9:1 LB

Contents

Preface

E ach time I read the following Scripture, a desire lingers in my heart to delve further into its meaning. Whatever prompts this desire stems from a far deeper inspiration than I can recognize. These words of Jesus from the Sermon on the Mount, really express how I feel in my own heart.

> Consider the lilies of the field, how they grow; they toil not, neither do they spin: And yet I say unto you, That even Solomon in all his glory was not arrayed like one of these. Wherefore, if God so clothe the grass of the field, which today is, and tomorrow is cast into the oven, shall He not much more clothe you, O ye of little faith?
>
> *Matthew 6:28–30*

For years I longed to write a book based on these beautiful words, but I could not incorporate my thoughts into enough material to fill a book. Only fragmented ideas with loose ends seemed to clutter my thinking. How to tie all the loose ends together was beyond my scope. I hoped to draw attention to similarities between plants and people in relation to environments and to establish how flowers exist in a state of contentment despite often seemingly hazardous surroundings.

When I read these words by Rev. Charles H. Spurgeon—"Sleepy Christian, thou art sleeping while souls are being lost."[1]—I felt an even stronger burden to give my testimony at the same time, but where and how to begin? I had never taken a course in creative writing.

Then one day I received in the mail an attractive card with a possibility thought imprinted on it from Dr. Robert H. Schuller of Garden Grove, California. It said, "There are infinite possibilities in little beginnings if God is in them."[2] That one sentence is packed with motivation, and it certainly moved me to action.

Dr. Schuller often says, "It is better to try something great and fail, than to try nothing at all and succeed." With this kind of encouragement and after much prayerful consideration, I seemed to get the green light to go ahead and at least make an attempt to put my thoughts into writing.

I have learned that the beauty of nature is truly in the eyes of the beholder. Not everyone notices a weed or hears a bird's song at a busy intersection. One has to constantly be looking and listening for nature's gifts. My efforts to learn more about plant life led me to the Queens Botanical Garden, the New York Botanical Garden in the Bronx, St. John's University library, and various local branch libraries and garden centers. Walks along country roads from early spring through late summer brought to my attention many of the lovely flowering weeds that we usually ignore. For example, all along our city streets and roadsides we find an abundance of chicory with its delicate pale blue-lilac flowers. The roots can be ground and used as an additive or substitute for coffee. The pink bouncing bets, also known as *soapworts*, grow between pavement and fences. They were used as detergent by early settlers because the leaves lather when squeezed in water.

Research into how plants adapt to environmental conditions confirmed many thoughts concerning my own experiences in

Christ over the past thirty years. Basically, plants struggle to survive in their little patch of ground. They have a strong will to live in spite of harsh elements, discouraging environment among choking weeds, tangled roots of larger plants, and trampling under foot of animals and people. Amazingly, they continue to flourish and spin in the sun as though they had no hindrance at all. We too must battle the "elements" that continually try our patience, the social problems that we encounter in our daily lives, and our own inner fears and frustrations. We can and we do survive because we have help from on high. The most difficult part (and I say this because I find it a hard rule to follow) is keeping our discouragements a private matter between God and ourselves (Matthew 6:6) and allowing others to see only the faith of God reflected in our face and not our hindrances.

The little plants neither fret nor worry, yet they fulfill the purpose of their existence, be it for food, medicine, or household products. Like the plants, we too were created to be useful, functioning, nurturing vessels. No matter how little it seems, we can make someone else's life a little brighter, even if we are hurting in the midst of extreme difficulties or hardships.

I did indeed "consider the lilies," and I wish to share some of these thoughts in the pages that follow. My idea started small, but with God's help a plan grew as my thoughts unfolded like the petals of a flower and as words flowed into my mind. This is my written testimony to a loving and caring Savior who never lets me down. Victory over anxiety is my theme. The credit and the glory go to the Lord who uses me as a vessel to serve Him however he may choose.

Acknowledgments

My sincere appreciation to the reference librarians at St. John's University Library, Jamaica, N.Y., and at the Flushing and Glen Oaks branches of the Queens Borough Public Libraries for assisting in my research. My appreciation also to the permissions editors of the publishing companies mentioned in the notes for their advice and assistance in the laborious task of seeking copyrights. Special thanks to Mary E. Kennan, Editor, Spectrum Books, for making this book possible, and to Stephanie Kiriakopoulos, her assistant, and to Claudia Citarella, production editor, for their guidance every step of the way. My thanks also to Susan Lacerte, horticulturist. I am grateful too, for all who work behind the scenes at Prentice-Hall, Inc.

> The Lord gave the word: great was the company of those that published it.
>
> *Psalm 68:11*

All Scripture references are taken from the King James Version unless otherwise stated. References marked NIV are given in the

New International Version (Grand Rapids, Mich.: Zondervan Bible Publishers, 1978), and those marked LB are given in the Living Bible Version (Wheaton, Ill.: Tyndale House, 1971).

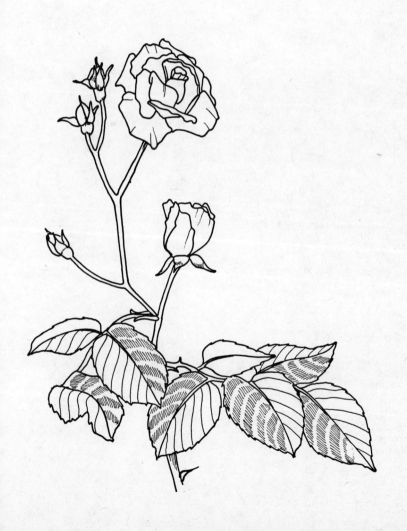

More precious than gold

Whenever I consider the lilies, my thoughts invariably focus on the graceful, white trumpet-shaped flower with delicate yellow shadings. These tall, elegant, white lilies, ever popular at Easter, grace the chancels of churches and adorn covers of magazines and religious literature during the Lenten season. They are abundantly displayed at garden centers in large clay pots with labels bearing the distinguished-sounding botanical name *Lilium longiflorum,* more commonly called the *Easter lily.*

> Consider the lilies of the field, how they grow; they toil not, neither do they spin: And yet I say unto you, That even Solomon in all his glory was not arrayed like one of these. Wherefore, if God so clothe the grass of the field, which today is, and tomorrow is cast into the oven, shall He not much more clothe you, O ye of little faith?
>
> *Matthew 6:28–30*

It may surprise you, as it did me, to know that when Jesus drew our attention to the lilies of the field, He was not referring to the lily as we know it today. Many researchers believe He might have been referring to the anemone, or windflower, that grew wild after the spring rains in Jerusalem. The word *anemone* comes from the Greek word *anemos,* meaning "wind." The flowers were given the name *windflower* because they thrived best in windy places. These flowers still bloom along the roadsides and in the plains and valleys in the holy land. Some authorities say Jesus was speaking of flowers in general when He said, "Consider the lilies of the field," but, regardless of which flower He meant, the message still applies.

When I gaze at the incredible beauty of any flower, my thoughts are fixed on the words spoken by Jesus in Matthew, chapter 6. He was teaching us that there was more to life than meat and more to the body than dress. If God clothes the flowers more regally than the richest king, without need for anxious labor on their part, think how much more He will care for us!

Food, clothing, and possessions alone do not constitute life, even though they are necessary and desirable. There are better and far more important things to seek after—God and His righteousness being the first desire (Matthew 6:33).

Try to remember a time when you visited a botanical garden or visualize in your mind the most breathtaking array of flowers you have ever seen. Perhaps you stood on a hillside or in a meadow where thousands of flowers bloomed in magnificent profusion. Were you not overwhelmed by their dazzling performance?

If you consider the lily or the rose or the lilac and marvel at the beauty of their colors, the intricately designed petals and fragrant perfume, you cannot deny the fact that only God could have patterned them. Some flowers have four petals and some have dozens, yet each one is an unparalleled masterpiece of creation.

Travel through picturesque countrysides in autumn, when the foliage is ablaze in spectacular shades of crimson, orange, gold, and brown. Can there be any doubt in your mind that God touched the earth and clothed it in awesome majesty? How wonderful are the works of the Lord!

The Word says that "Solomon in all his glory was not arrayed like one of these" (Matthew 6:29). King Solomon's wealth and grandeur are described in detail in I Kings 10:14, 18, 21, 22, 24–26:

> Now the weight of gold that came to Solomon in one year was six hundred threescore and six talents of gold, ... Moreover the king made a great throne of ivory, and overlaid it with the best gold.... And all King Solomon's drinking vessels were of gold, and all the vessels of the house of the forest of Lebanon were of pure gold.... Once in three years came the navy of Tharshish, bringing gold, and silver, ivory, and apes, and peacocks.... And all the earth sought to Solomon, to hear his wisdom, which God had put in his heart. And they brought every man his present, vessels of silver, and vessels of gold, and garments, and armour, and spices, horses, and mules.... and he had a thousand and four hundred chariots, and twelve thousand horsemen.... And the king made silver to be in Jerusalem as stones.

Yes, indeed, King Solomon was a very rich man! This is but a small portion of the revenue and splendor bestowed on him by God, for I have only quoted it in part. Yet Jesus found the flowers of the field more worthy to be compared to the king's riches, fame, and glory; and you and I to be more precious than both.

> Wherefore, if God so clothe the grass of the field, which today is, and tomorrow is cast into the oven, shall he not much more clothe you, O ye of little faith?
>
> *Matthew 6:30*

Dwelling in perfect peace

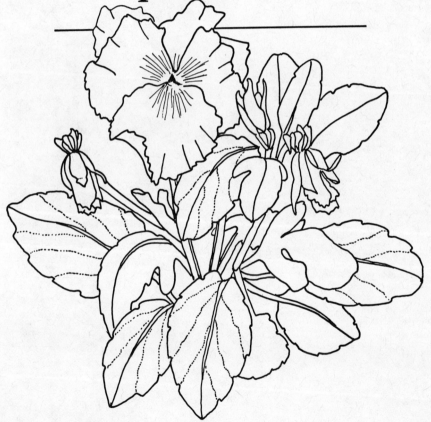

Since the beginning of time, flowers have had universal appeal as gifts because there is an enchanting quality about them. Special occasions such as proms and anniversaries call for floral corsages. Bridal parties are resplendent with bouquets, and dining tables are enhanced by centerpieces.

Flowers and plants are splendid gifts to bring or send to hospital patients. You will notice on Valentine's Day, Mother's Day, and at Easter time, florists do a bonanza business. Evidently, flowers are the most welcome of all presents. Watch a woman's eyes light up with delight when she receives flowers. She gently caresses the velvet-soft petals and instinctively holds the flowers to her nose as though drinking in the fragrance and beauty.

Flowers were used as national symbols,[3] and, based on folklore and mythology, they conveyed certain feelings: pansies stand for thoughts, daisies for innocence, anemone for expectation, jasmine for admirability, and heather for solitude, to name just a few. The language of flowers is called *florigraphy.*

Gardening seems to have a therapeutic effect on many people who are infirm or who for some reason are unable to do heavier work. The task is pleasant and the results rewarding.

Retirees often turn to serious planting, spending more and more time in their garden. It is well worth the effort when they can sit and relax to enjoy the fruit of their labor.

Floral arrangements in a myriad of colors give great pleasure to young and old alike in flower shows, gardens, and window boxes. Even a single blossom in a homely jar in an office becomes the focal point of the day, commented on by all who pass, bringing a few moments of joy to the beholder.

Flowers have been found growing where we would least expect them. In spite of the fact that they are incredibly fragile, they are a hardy lot and adapt to extreme temperatures. In the arctic regions, for instance, kaleidoscopic colors of yellow avens, buttercups, arctic poppies, and cinquefoil decorate the land. Colonies of bluebells, purple saxifrage, red-pink louseworts, and arctic bell heather with their little white, bell-shaped flowers carpet the thawing tundras for several weeks in springtime.

> Showers soften the earth, melting the clods and causing seeds to sprout across the land.
>
> *Psalm 65:10 LB*

Low-growing species that inhabit the area have shallow, wide-spreading roots; for just inches below the surface the earth is frozen solid with permafrost and inches above the air is freezing and the winds bitter; much too cold for them to survive if they were taller. As the sun warms the face of the frozen earth, flowers, lichten, and mosses thrive by hugging the ground. They derive warmth and shelter from the sun's rays, unperturbed by the hostile weather surrounding them.

Often I have kept geraniums blooming all winter in pots on sunny window ledges. Outside the temperature may be almost zero, but the warmth of the sun through the glass keeps them alive as though it were summer. Just an inch away, on the other side of the glass, the plants could certainly freeze to death, but they do not borrow trouble by worrying about what "could be."

Exquisite orchids grow high in the trees in steaming tropical forests. Since the forest floor is bogged with swamps, mud, and decaying matter, there is little access to the soil. Very little sunlight penetrates through the dense vegetation to reach the ground. Only high in the treetops can the orchids catch rain water and glimpses of sun trickling through the heavy canopy of leaves and branches. The source of their nutrients is the organic matter that collects high up in the barks of trees. How do the orchids get up there? The breeze carries the tiny seeds through the air.

The ecological environment of the forest is unsuitable for human habitation, yet it produces rare and beautiful exotic plants that are well adapted to live in oppressively hot and humid climates.

When you see pictures of the hot, dry, burning desert, you feel certain that it would be impossible for anything to grow in the sand, but all desert plants have fascinating ways of adapting to life with very little water. The most popular resident is the cactus, which contains its own built-in water storage. The spongelike tissues absorb water, while the very thick, succulent stems prevent moisture loss through evaporation. The cactus has no leaves, thereby preventing even more water from escaping. Even the showy white, red, and purple cup-shaped blossoms nestled in the impenetrable spiny surface of the cactus are a miracle of creation. The waxy texture of their flower petals is uniquely designed to help retain moisture. Most of the desert plants have shallow but extensive root systems designed to absorb as much moisture as possible from the ground. During drought the plants remain dormant and reactivate to soak up water when rain falls.

The name *mesquite bush* may have a familiar ring. These spiny bushes and trees have tap roots extending twenty-five to seventy-five feet, penetrating deep into the ground in search of water.

In some parts of the desert, after a brief rainstorm, thousands of dormant wildflowers miraculously spring forth into brilliant gardens. They have been waiting a long time for the water. What a thrill it must be to see fragrant sand verbena, yellow dwarf sunflowers, golden poppies, and purple owlclover come to life and to see the delicate sego lily blooming in that dry land under conditions that would cause other life to perish.

> Who cuts a channel for the torrents of rain, and a path for the thunderstorm, to water a land where no man lives, a desert with no one in it, to satisfy a desolate wasteland and make it sprout with grass?

Job 38:25–27 NIV

Brief torrential rains in a desert in Western United States trigger powerful flash floods. With incredible speed and deafening noise, the excess rain water rushes down through the arroyos, or gullies, carrying boulders as if they were pebbles. The runoff disappears into a canyon and eventually settles into a quiet pool. One would expect to find sagebrush and cacti, but to see red monkey flowers, ferns, and other vegetation growing in these cool ravines is an unexpected treat.

Can you see how this might resemble a pattern that all too often occurs in our own lives? There may be long, dry periods of unchanging humdrum existence—go to work, come home, look forward to uneventful weekends, then back to work where the days seem so long. For weeks, months, and even years there can be long dry spells when nothing interesting takes place. Then, suddenly, one day something traumatic happens and releases a whole chain of events, perhaps good, perhaps not so good. How often do you hear people say, "When it rains, it pours" or "It's just one thing after another"? Like a flood in a desert, we are deluged with trials or joys showered on us all at once until it seems we can hardly bear any more. Then they reach a peak, and everything comes to rest for another interminable period of sameness. Thank God for the quiet times. How much more we appreciate them after the storms. Though we may be dismayed and frightened by them, remember it takes the storms to make the desert bloom. The author of this poem said it so well.

My life was a desert full of sand,
The sun burned down to scorch the land,
No vegetation grew in me,
Just stones, and sand, and misery.

But then there came a healing rain:
God set my gloomy heart aflame,
And, from the burning sand, there grew
Green grass, and flowers of every hue.

He watered it with magic love,
And tuned my heart to look above,
And, in the sunshine of His smile,
My empty life became worthwhile.

He caused the sand, once in repose,
In love, to blossom like the rose,
The barren earth to sprout, and grow,
Where e'er His Living Waters flow!

W. R. Goodman, "Desert Sand"[4]

You will find flowers growing in the most unlikely places—between paved walks, on the edge of rooftops, in splits in tarred and macadam roadways, and in garbage-strewn lots. Broken glass, tin cans, rubber tires, and assorted litter do not deter these spunky plants from reaching their ultimate goal. In their relentless attempts to seek sunlight, they will bend out of shape and stretch their stems to the limit to surmount every obstacle that blocks their path. In spite of their loathsome habitats, they finally flower and glow like precious jewels in the sun.

I read about one feisty little flower that "had grown up to two feet high, between the horses' path and the wheel-track. An inch more to right or left had sealed its fate, or an inch higher; and yet it lived to flourish as much as if it had a thousand acres of untrodden space around it, and never knew the danger it incurred."[5]

It is a most amazing discovery when you find a solitary flower growing in a crack in a rock. Can any environment be more hostile or undesirable? Yet, if undisturbed, the plant lives its life span and remains beautiful. Surely God takes care of the tiniest, loneliest flower, dresses it splendidly, and finds it a home.

Perhaps Alfred, Lord Tennyson must have entertained similar thoughts when he wrote,

> Flower in the crannied wall
> I pluck you out of the crannies
> I hold you here, root and all, in my hand.
> Little flower—but if I could understand
> What you are, root and all, and all in all,
> I should know what God and man is.
>
> *Alfred, Lord Tennyson,*
> *"Flower in the Crannied Wall"*[6]

A tiny flower called *saxifrage,* sometimes known as *rock-breaker,* grows in the crevices of rocks. This remarkable flower adapts easily to inaccessible places such as rock slides by taking root in the soil that collects in narrow openings. Tiny plants have been known to literally crack a rock as the root begins to grow.

Speaking of rock-breakers, perhaps you know someone whom you care about very much, but whose heart is as hard as stone toward God? Try as you may, you have never been able to get through to tell that dear one about Jesus. You almost want to give up trying, since it appears impossible; but it is not impossible with God. All you can do is keep on planting seeds of love. One day one of the seeds you sow will take root, and God will crack that heart of stone. Perhaps you will not be the one to lead that person to Christ, but your prayers must never cease. A mother may pray for years for her child to come to the Lord or a wife may pray for her husband, but someone else may deliver that soul-saving message and give the invitation that will lead to a changed life. Your prayers have not been in vain. Don't stop when you think you are praying to no avail. Just one seed is all it takes; the Holy Spirit will nurture it with water and sunshine. Some of the seeds sown will have "rock-breaking" power.

All through the pouring rain, flowers droop their heads and bend to touch the earth. When the sun shines, their unharmed petals open once again, refreshed and sparkling, ready to begin a new day. A broken leaf or bent stem does not deter their growth. In the growing process the little flowers lift their nodding heads, reaching and stretching toward the light, unmindful of perils surrounding them. Their only concern is receiving warmth and nourishment from the sun, rain, and earth. In return they give beauty and gladness of heart.

My favorite example of flowers living in complete serenity and contentment are the pansies. Even when they occupy the humblest of living quarters, pansies still charm the viewer. By their very existence they radiate a warming glow that seems to say, "We have survived the chill of early spring, the onslaught of heavy rains, and the shock of being moved from seed tray to earth bed with rough hands and steel trowel. This is where we have been planted and will remain, so that we will shine and sparkle and make this place as beautiful for you as we know how." No matter how many burdens weigh you down, one look at the charming pansies will bring a smile to your lips and a sparkle to your eyes. In early England, they were called *heart's-ease,* a very fitting name. They appear to have faces that look up and smile at you as if to assure you that all is well.

This kind of victory over anxiety is what Paul meant when he said, "I have learned, in whatsoever state I am, therewith to be content" (Philippians 4:11).

Ask what ye will

In the dictionary *anxiety* is defined as "some uncertain event that disturbs the mind and keeps it in a state of painful uneasiness." No one had more reason to suffer anxiety than Paul. He was in prison when he wrote his letter to the Philippians. More than once he was hunted, beaten, and thrown into cold, dark prisons without food or clothes, yet for Jesus' sake he was willing to suffer persecutions. Deep in his soul he knew the secret of being content, no matter what the outward conditions were.

I know what it is to be in need, and I know what it is to have plenty. I have learned the secret of being content in any and every situation, whether well fed or hungry, whether living in plenty or in want. I can do everything through him who gives me strength.

Philippians 4:12, 13 NIV

The definition of *content* given in the dictionary is "to make quiet; to satisfy the mind; comfortable; to make easy; passive; ready." Paul exemplified all of these things. He knew that as long as he kept his eyes focused on Christ and not the afflictions,

Jesus would give him strength and would carry him through any ordeal. Paul shares with us his secret of God's peace.

> Do not be anxious about anything, but in everything, by prayer and petition, with thanksgiving, present your requests to God. And the peace of God, which transcends all understanding, will guard your hearts and your minds in Christ Jesus.
>
> *Philippians 4:6, 7 NIV*

Yes, Paul was acquainted with acute physical and mental suffering. Even if he did not recount in detail the terrible tortures he lived through, you only have to read between the lines to imagine the pain he endured during his ministry.

Let me tell you briefly something about this man Paul. Perhaps then you can appreciate even more the significance of his words of contentment in the midst of any situation. In his own words, he was a Jew of Tarsus, born to a wealthy family of tentmakers, who were members of the very strict religious sect called *Pharisees*. This young Pharisee, whose Jewish name was Saul, was a brilliant student, educated in Jerusalem under the distinguished rabbinical teacher, Gamaliel (see Acts 18:3; 22:3; 26:4, 5).

Saul was a zealous Jewish scholar, trained in tradition and culture of Old Testament Scripture. He spoke Greek, Aramaic, and Latin and had an excellent knowledge of the Law. His occupation as a tentmaker enabled him to support himself and his associates later in his ministry (Acts 20:34).

As a devout Jew, Saul's beliefs clashed violently with those of the Christians. He refused to believe what the Christians were preaching, that Jesus of Nazareth was the Messiah. He led the campaign to persecute the Christians. Men and women were dragged from their homes and cast into prison if they were caught preaching.

Saul even went so far as to seek permission from the high priest to go to Damascus and bring prisoners back to Jerusalem (Acts 9:1, 2). However, the Lord God had other plans. On the way to Damascus, Saul was suddenly blinded by a great light from heaven and he "heard a voice saying unto him, Saul, Saul, why persecutest thou me? And he said, Who art thou, Lord? And the Lord answered, I am Jesus whom thou persecutest" (Acts 9:4, 5). Saul fell on the ground, trembling with fear and cried, "Lord, what wilt thou have me to do?" (Acts 9:6).

The men who journeyed with Saul obeyed God's instructions to lead the sightless Saul by the hand to Damascus. There God sent the disciple, Ananias, to minister to Saul so that he might receive his sight and be filled with the Holy Ghost. Ananias was well aware of the harm Saul had done to the saints in Jerusalem. He was afraid to face Saul, and who could blame him? But the Lord assured Ananias by saying of Saul,

> Go thy way: for he is a chosen vessel unto me, to bear my name before the Gentiles, and kings, and the children of Israel. For I will show him how great things he must suffer for my name's sake.
>
> *Acts 9:15, 16*

Ananias obeyed and ministered to Saul. Saul confessed his belief in Jesus, received his sight, and was baptized. After his conversion, Saul was willing to give his life for the very thing he had previously fought against so vehemently. He immediately began by preaching in synagogues and to the Gentiles that Jesus truly is the Son of God (see Acts 9:20–22).

This man, who was a murderer of Christians and who watched, without blinking an eye, as young Stephen was stoned to death; this man, with a remarkable memory and vast knowledge of the Old Testament Scriptures, was chosen by God to become one of the greatest missionaries and evangelists of all time. You see how Saul, also named Paul (Acts 13:9), a once comfortable, wealthy young man, had to be blinded, humbled, broken, and made into another vessel before God could use him effectively. For the rest of his life Paul loved and served God, and it was no easy task, for he did suffer for Christ's sake. He traveled on long missionary journeys as an ambassador, establishing and uniting the Church wherever he went. Often he journeyed on foot in winter and at times he had to flee after severe beatings were administered to him, without waiting to recover from his wounds. He trained faithful men and women as apostles to spread the Gospel throughout the world. He wrote the epistles in the New Testament, exhorting, instructing, and comforting the brethren. In the epistles, Paul declared the believer's hope, the second coming of Christ, and the doctrine concerning the believer's manner of living. He was careful to practice what he preached. Paul would not tell others to "be content with such things as ye have" (Hebrews 13:5) without setting an example of such behavior himself (II Thessalonians 3:9, 10; I Timothy 1:15, 16).

He was not in the best of health to begin with during some of his incarcerations. By his own admission in II Corinthians 11:23–27, he had been starved and scourged till he bled, his clothes were taken away, and he was thrown into cold, damp dungeons with only the bare floor to sit on. Besides all of these torments, he was plagued by another "thorn in the flesh" (II Corinthians 12:7), which was perhaps an infirmity brought on by years of torture to his body, some birth deformity, or maybe some external harassment. Nevertheless, in his weakened, pitiful condition, Paul still prayed for his friends, sang hymns, praised God, and rejoiced that he knew Jesus. One night he witnessed to his jailor in Philippi, thus converting him to Christ.

I find it so amazing that, in spite of all his suffering, Paul could still say, "I have learned, in whatsoever state I am, therewith to be content" (Philippians 4:11).

This is exactly the kind of faith that Jesus was talking about in the Sermon on the Mount.

> ... do not worry about your life, what you will eat or drink; or about your body, what you will wear. Is not life more important than food? ... Look at the birds of the air; they do not sow or reap or store away in barns, and yet your heavenly Father feeds them. Are you not much more valuable than they? ... Therefore do not worry about tomorrow, for tomorrow will worry about itself. Each day has enough trouble of its own.
>
> *Matthew 6:25, 26, 34 NIV*

Where else can you find a greater example of the embodiment of faith than in children? These little ones do not spend their time worrying about their needs. They leave that to their parents. Listen to their conversation, especially at Christmas time: "What are you getting for Christmas?" "I am getting a doll and my brother is getting electric trains." "How do you know that?" "Because I asked Santa Claus!" It is as simple as that. She asked and then knew without a doubt that she would be getting what she so desired.

I remember when I was very small, my mother asked me what I wanted for Christmas. There was a little China tea set in the store window that I wanted. Each time I passed the window, I would tell my friends, "See what I am getting for Christmas," as though it were already mine. I knew I would soon have it because mother said so, and I did get the dishes just as I expected.

> If ye then, being evil, know how to give good gifts unto your children, how much more shall your Father which is in heaven give good things to them that ask him?
>
> *Matthew 7:11*

> Therefore take no thought, saying, What shall we eat? or, What shall we drink? or, Wherewithal shall we be clothed? ... for your heavenly father knoweth that ye have need of all these things.
>
> *Matthew 6:31, 32*

God knows all of our desires, all of our requests for healing, and all of our financial needs, but He still expects us to tell Him. Then, after we ask Him, we must in faith believe that our prayers have already been answered, just as children ask their parents and then forget about it, knowing they will get what was asked for.

> And this is the confidence that we have in him, that, if we ask any thing according to his will, he heareth us; and if we know that he hear us, whatsoever we ask, we know that we have the petitions that we desired of Him.
>
> *I John 5:14, 15*

It took me a very long time to realize that "according to His will" meant that I must tell God my needs and then trust Him to answer in His own way. Even when I do not always get what I want, it is for my best interest. God knows me better than I know myself. I am fickle; what I want today, I may not want tomorrow. My parents knew that—they did not always give me everything I asked.

When I accept God's will as my will, when I stop being restless and impatient for answers to prayer, then I will experience real peace. This resignation, this surrendering and allowing God to carry me, I believe, is God's will.

Oh, I still tell God my desires and very often He answers my prayer requests, but I am learning to trust His timing and His judgment of what is right or wrong for me.

Archbishop Francois Fenelon wrote in one of his spiritual letters, "We can learn a lesson from babies. Babies own nothing. They treat diamonds and apples alike. Be a babe. Have nothing of your own. It all belongs to God anyway."[7] You may see a baby fret, but you will never see a baby losing sleep by worrying about what tomorrow will bring. This same childlike faith is all that God requires of us. Jesus said, "Except ye be converted, and become as little children, ye shall not enter into the kingdom of heaven" (Matthew 18:3).

Anxiety, when prolonged, can only create problems, manifesting itself in poor appetite, lack of sleep, and eventually poor health. Almost everyone comes to grips with anxiety at some time. What is important is that you do not allow the disquieting thoughts to take root. They will surely rob you of your peace. Anxiety stems from lack of faith in God's care for you.

Be assured that He will always be very close to your side while you are going through troubled times. Paul said to the people of Athens, and it is true of us today, "He is not far from each one of us" (Acts 17:27 NIV). Knowing that He is always near is a comforting thought. You can turn to Him in the midst of your most disturbing moments, and there you will find a peace that you never knew existed; the same peace and security a little boy feels when a loving father gathers him up in strong arms to comfort him.

The author of the following verse knew well how to deal with anxious thoughts:

Whate'er the care which breaks thy rest
Whate'er the wish that swells thy breast.
Spread before God that wish, that care
And change anxiety into prayer.

Jane Crewdson[8]

Read what St. Francis de Sales said about anxiety:

Do not look forward to the changes and chances of this life in fear; rather look to them with full hope that, as they arise, God, whose you are, will deliver you out of them. He has kept you hitherto, do you but hold fast to His dear Hand, and He will lead you safely through all things: and, when you cannot stand, He will bear you in His arms.[9]

There is great assurance in knowing you have a heavenly Father to turn to and a protective hand to cling to.

When we were little children, we were never anxious about where our next meal was coming from or if we would have something cool to drink in the summer or something warm to wear in the winter. We never gave it a second thought, simply because we knew that all our needs were taken care of by our parents. The older I get, the more I reminisce on those carefree days of my childhood. Life was safe and sheltered beneath my parents' roof. How blessed we would be if we could feel that same sense of security under God's sheltering wing.

Ask Him to replace your anxiety with contentment and trust Him for an answer. He will give you peace that transcends all understanding.

What things soever ye desire, when ye pray, believe that ye receive them, and ye shall have them.

Mark 11:24

For
everything
there is
a purpose

There are millions of flowers blooming on earth at the same time, and each individual blossom has a distinct purpose and beauty all its own.

Then God said, "I give you every seed-bearing plant on the face of the whole earth and every tree that has fruit with seed in it. They will be yours for food. And to all the beasts of the earth and all the birds of the air and all the creatures that move on the ground—everything that has the breath of life in it—I give every green plant for food." And it was so.

Genesis 1:29, 30 NIV

According to this verse, the prime purpose of vegetation for man, bird, and beast is to be a source of food.

Through the centuries men have discovered that the plant world yields other ingredients for sustaining life. The Indians and early settlers used the stems, leaves, flowers, and roots of plants to cure stomach ailments, pains, and sore throats. They also made teas, tonics, and various household products, such as candles from the waxy bayberries, threads, soaps, and dyes.

Researchers in pharmaceutical laboratories have uncovered sedatives, dyes, stimulants, drugs, cosmetics, perfumes, and gums in the botanical world. Lavender oil contains a cosmetic germicide and is also used for making perfumes. Other flowers such as the jasmine, rose, heliotrope, hyacinth, and violet contain oil in their petals from which natural perfumes are made.

Try to imagine the incomparable heavenly fragrance of honeysuckle drifting gently in the air on a summer evening. The function of the perfume is not only to delight us, but to attract bees, butterflies, and other insects that go about pollinating the flowers or gathering honey as they stop to visit.

Seeds from the mustard, coriander, nutmeg, and pepper plants provide us with fragrant aromatic spices. Herbs such as dill, anise, mint, and sage supply us with culinary flavoring. The vanilla orchid bears pods used for flavoring desserts. Grains from barley, wheat, and rye, which were cultivated for making bread since antiquity, still supply us with breakfast cereals and bread.

The common dandelion has so many uses. Its seeds are food for the birds. The leaves, rich in vitamins, are used in salads; and wines are made from the flowers. Even the roots are useful; they contain a drug for treating liver ailments.

From the stamen of the crocuslike saffron flower comes the dye in orange food coloring, the costliest to produce. Dyes and stains are extracted from the dried orange safflower. Blue dye is manufactured from the indigo plant. Pioneer women used pokeberries and elderberries to dye their fabrics.

Oil is extracted from the flax seed, and the fibrous stems provide threads for bookbinding and clothing. Linen was mentioned often in the Old Testament, and since linen is made from flax, we know that this plant has a long history. Egyptian tombs are decorated with drawings of flax. Archaeologists have unearthed remains of clothing and fish nets of linen used in the Stone Age. In Genesis 41:42, Pharoah arrayed Joseph in vestures of fine linen. The sacred raiment of the priests and the curtains for the Tabernacle in the wilderness were made of fine linen (Exodus 26:1; 28:6). Jesus' burial cloth was made of fine linen (Matthew 27:59).

The tall Asiatic hemp plant yields fibers used for making rope and sailcloth. Medicines were extracted from the cassia plant as far back as Old Testament days when Moses was erecting the Tabernacle (see Exodus 30:24–25). The pleasant-tasting coriander seed mentioned in Exodus 16:31 also had a medicinal use in the Holy Land.

Some of the drugs that were derived from the plants in ancient times are still used today. Morphine and codeine are two of the principal active substances from the opium poppy indigenous to Asia Minor; digitalis, a cardiac stimulant, is a derivative of the foxglove plant. Another drug, hashish, is produced from flowers and leaves of the hemp plant native to Asia. A substance for treating burns comes from the aloe plant.

Perhaps you have some therapeutic remedies of your own, handed down from your grandmother. My mother sometimes brewed tea from fennel seeds as a remedy for stomach aches.

Before any one of the products mentioned here could be made available to us, part of the plant had to undergo some sort of processing. They had to be pressed for oils, dried and crushed for herbs, and put through the fire for stains and dyes. All had to be broken down in some way or other before becoming useful ingredients.

> The earth is satisfied with the fruit of thy works. He causeth the grass to grow for the cattle, and herb for the service of man: that he may bring forth food out of the earth; And wine that maketh glad the heart of man, and oil to make his face to shine, and bread which strengtheneth man's heart. The trees of the Lord are full of sap; the cedars of Lebanon, which he hath planted; Where the birds make their nests: as for the stork the fir trees are her house.
>
> *Psalm 104:13–16*

Consider the trees. What a marvelous act of creation when you stop to think of them! Can you imagine how much would be lacking in our lives if there were no trees? We depend on them for utensils, tools, housing, furniture, and a host of other essential items—from the pencil in our hand and the paper we write on, to the roof over our head. From one generation to the next, trees grow and continue to provide man with most basic necessities. What an ingenious idea it was to slice trees into boards for lumber to build homes.

Wood pulp is the raw material used in manufacturing paper products. Twenty years ago it required about 140 acres of pulpwood timber to produce a 128-page edition of a Sunday newspaper with a circulation of 1 million.

What would we ever do without trees? Just imagine all the products derived from these creations and all the jobs that the lumber industry provides. How blessed we are that in this generation there is better forest management, modern conservation methods, new systems for ensuring future timber, and paper recycling. Today more trees are being replanted than are being cut down.

While the shade offers protection from the sun, the leaves help to purify the air we breathe. Trees provide sanctuary for many of God's creatures. Songbirds, owls, squirrels, monkeys, mice, insects, and the tiniest aphids live and feed among the branches.

Cherry, pecan, and cedar wood are used for making furniture, and fine musical instruments are made from mahogany. Because cedar contains a natural moth repellant, it is ideal for chests, drawers, and closets. The reddish-hued wood is durable and aromatic, perfect for storing woolen garments. Mother once owned a cedar chest, and we used to love the woodsy fragrance that escaped whenever she opened it. Toy airplanes are made from the soft, light weight basswood. Rounded boat bottoms, railroad ties, and water tanks are made from cypress trees. Many of the products that were made from wood have been replaced by plastics, but there are still some things that can only come from a tree.

My favorite is the deliciously scented pine, especially at Christmas time. The gaily decorated Christmas tree has something in common with a birthday cake. For example, when a loved one has a birthday, we celebrate by lighting candles on a lavishly decorated cake. Lighted candles make the occasion cheerful and festive. At that special moment, when surrounded by family and close friends, the celebrity feels an overwhelming sense of love. The Christmas tree plays a similar part in the celebration of Jesus' birth. When the decorations and tinsel are hung and the lights go on at last in the darkened room, all radiant and blinking, my heart lights up with joy and wonder. Happy Birthday, Jesus! What a grand and glorious role for the pine tree.

These are just some of the many ways that trees serve man. The list could go on and on, filling volumes of books on library shelves. Every wooden article we own was once a live tree.

You may be convinced by now, from what you have just read and from what you already know, that all plants fulfill some purpose, but what about the cactus? What possible use could it serve, standing in the desert's agonizing heat with very little rain? If anything had a reason to suffer anxiety, it would be the cactus, which, from all appearances, seems to have nothing going for it and everything against it. Some are even quite grotesque and ugly, especially the Joshua tree.

The giant saguaro cactus plant, which grows in the blistering heat of the Sonoran Desert, is an engineering feat. During the long periods between waterings, the cactus shrivels up. Then, when the rains come, it absorbs great quantities of water, nearly doubling its weight. Some of these massive plants weigh several tons after drinking in enough moisture to last throughout the next long period of drought. The saguaro cactus is created with a system of expandable ridges to allow for this swelling. This is the same principle that builders incorporate into bridges, enabling them to expand in the heat.

The spines or thorns on the saguaro, which may be an inch or more in length and all the ridges, actually cast shadows on the plant so that, no matter which direction the sun falls, a part of the plant is always partially shaded. Some of these giants grow as high as fifty feet tall. The wooden skeletons that support the plants have been used as building materials for furniture, fences, corrals, and various parts of homes. Seeds from the saguaro fruit were ground into meal for baking, and the pulp was used for making candy. Cattle, birds, burros, and rodents feed on the cacti and the fruit that drops to the ground. Those animals that can, will climb up after the fruit.

Nesting holes carved in the saguaro by gila woodpeckers are air-conditioned, insulated by the thick pulpy walls of the plant. Cactus wrens, white-winged doves, gilded flickers, elf owls, screech owls, and more than twenty species of birds live in and among the various cactus plants, protected from predators by thorns. Lovely flowers grow among the spines. Water stored in the barrel cactus can provide a drink for a thirsty traveler. By cutting a piece from the top and squeezing the pulp, it is possible to catch the liquid that drips from it. No doubt about it, the cactus is a very useful and necessary plant.

All of these miracles in the plant world only serve to reaffirm my faith in God, the Creator of the universe.

> The heavens declare the glory of God; and the firmament showeth his handiwork. Day unto day uttereth speech, and night unto night showeth knowledge. There is no speech nor language, where their voice is not heard."
>
> *Psalm 19:1–3*

Albeit the jungles, the deserts, or the arctic, His Hand touches all the earth. It is not "Mother Nature," but Father God who paints and decorates the everchanging cloud formations, the seasonal colors, the fantastic sunrises, and the romantic sunsets.

Ralph Waldo Emerson said, "All I have seen teaches me to trust the Creator for all I have not seen."[10]

Lately I have heard so many people say, "I have no time to stop and smell the roses." Well, take time, it will refresh you. God surrounded us with so much beauty on the earth, but too often it is taken for granted and goes unnoticed. One only has to stop and take a moment to be aware and enjoy the pleasures that they afford.

Occasionally, when I have a morning or afternoon free, I take a walk to the garden center near my home, just to browse. The greenhouse and the outdoor garden are stocked with an abundance of plants and flowers of every description and color.

I never have a problem deciding what to bring someone when I visit or to give someone for a birthday. A plant is always a welcome gift, and at the same time it gives me an excuse to enjoy every seasonal display at the center from spring through winter. My favorite gift is usually the prayer plant. At night all the leaves point upward, and they seem to take on the appearance of praying hands.

Lovely flower, what is your purpose? your function? Not only are you here to beautify the earth, but you have a job to do, a task to perform, a reason for being.

> As the rain and the snow come down from heaven, and do not return to it without watering the earth and making it bud and flourish, so that it yields seed for the sower and bread for the eater, so is my word that goes out from my mouth: It will not return to me empty, but will accomplish what I desire and achieve the purpose for which I sent it.
>
> *Isaiah 55:10, 11 NIV*

Every vessel God created serves a purpose, however seemingly obscure, useless, unattractive, despised, or lowly. It is God's earth. He placed everything and everyone here for a purpose, including you. God makes no mistakes. There is a job to be done by you and a reason for your being.

> To every thing there is a season, and a time to every purpose under the heaven.
>
> *Ecclesiastes 3:1*

In the garden

Flowers glistening and dancing in the sun have inspired poets throughout the ages. William Wordsworth loved to stroll in his garden and the surrounding rustic countryside near his cottage home. It was there that he received inspiration for many of his works, including this lovely poem about daffodils written in 1804:

> I wandered lonely as a cloud
> That floats on high o'er vales and hills,
> When all at once I saw a crowd,
> A host, of golden daffodils:
> Beside the lake, beneath the trees,
> Fluttering and dancing in the breeze.
>
> *William Wordsworth,*
> *"I Wandered Lonely As a Cloud"*[11]

I learned this poem in first grade and have loved it ever since. The last verse is almost a reflection of my own thoughts, but I could never express it as well as the author:

For oft, when on my couch I lie
In vacant or in pensive mood,
They flash upon that inward eye
Which is the bliss of solitude;
And then my heart with pleasure fills,
And dances with the daffodils.

William Wordsworth,
"I Wandered Lonely As a Cloud"[12]

Like Wordsworth, perhaps we all cherish one particular moment that flashes before our "inward eye," bringing with it pleasant thoughts. Whenever we have a dark, dismal winter day here in New York, my mind reverts back to a pleasant moment on a beach at Montauk Point. The day was warm and sunny. The mood was one of complete peace and serenity. The water was azure blue with gentle white caps, and the beach was white and rock-strewn, with waves rhythmically splashing on the shore. Colorful fishing boats were returning with their catches displayed along the sides. Gulls were gracefully circling and diving, and their cries were part of that lovely scene I engraved on my mind and tucked away for a rainy, snowy day.

Some of my most pleasant thoughts also stem from moments I spent walking in gardens. There has hardly been a poet or songwriter whose lyrics did not include references to flowers and gardens. No doubt even you have often quoted the familiar line from Shakespeare's *Romeo and Juliet,* "That which we call a rose by any other name would smell as sweet."[13] Peruse through a book of verse and you will discover graphic passages depicting the poet's reflections on boughs of cherry blossoms, roses in bloom, bleeding hearts, and violets. Amy Lowell reminisces about "Lilacs ... everywhere in this my New England,"[14] and Robert Frost recollects "Birches ... loaded with ice a sunny winter morning."[15] All of these lyrics undoubtedly bring to mind some of your own delightful childhood memories.

Certain flowers often bring back memories of times past. Most people seem interested when the subject comes up in conversation. They are ready to share an experience they had in raising a particular plant. While discussing some of the unusual places we discovered plants growing, my friend remembered an incident during World War II when she was a U.S. Army nurse serving in England. The sight of tiny green plants appearing on top of rubble heaps so soon after the bombings left a significant impression in her mind. In the midst of the terrible devastation and destruction surrounding her, the new growth was, to her, symbolic of new life. Here was the assurance of a new beginning. The sprouting plants seemed to promise hope for the future. Their arrival on the scene was like a breath of fresh air sweeping through the smoke and cinders of a war-torn city.

My interest in flowers began when I was very, very young, even before I went to school. I grew up in a tenement house in the South Bronx, and there were no trees on our street, only bricks, sidewalks, and cobblestones. The only garden we owned was mother's flower pots on the fire escape, blooming with petunias, begonias, and portulacas. We planted anything that would grow—sweet potatoes with their long, scrawny vines; carrot tops, and even onions that had already started to sprout in the bag. Mother had one huge flower pot containing a plant called *hen and chickens* that seemed to live forever. There was always a solitary red geranium on a fire escape window across the alley in the backyard. At Easter time our neighbors showed off foil-wrapped, potted blue hydrangeas, white lilies, or pink hyacinths on their window sills.

In early grade school we bought flower seed packets for a penny and narcissus bulbs to be planted at home and brought back on a given date to be judged "best flower" in a contest. Although I succeeded in growing a white narcissus and carried it proudly to school, I never won a prize.

Nearly every Sunday during the summer of our growing-up years, Mom would pack a lunch after church and Dad would take us all on a long subway ride to the end of the line and then on a very long hike through the open meadows and through the woods. My brother and I were able to walk, but Mom had to carry our baby sister. Dad carried the food and sometimes had to carry me when the brush was too tall and the bugs bothered me. I

41

would cry a lot when the mosquitos left big welts all over my arms and legs. Dad would make a cross in the welts by pressing his thumbnail into them. He said that was supposed to make the poison come out and stop the itching, but it only itched more. I still have a habit of making that little cross on a mosquito bite, even though I know it does nothing to help.

These excursions went on week after week, year after year. Dad liked walking through narrow paths in the woods while carrying a long twig. He would stop while he pointed out some particular plant or weed. That is how my love of flowers got started.

Each Sunday I would gather a bouquet of wild flowers or weeds if they were pretty enough and carry them all the way home on the long subway ride and put them in a milk bottle on our kitchen table. One week it would be buttercups. The way we identified this enameled-looking yellow flower was to hold one under our chin. If the yellow reflected on our chin, Dad said it meant we liked butter. Since we all liked butter and the yellow always reflected on our chin, we really believed his story.

Another week we would come upon a field of hundreds of violets, which made up my lavish bouquet to take home. Each week I would pick something different—wild iris, daffodils, Queen Anne's lace, black-eyed susans, and butter-and-eggs (a weed with attractive yellow-orange blossoms, which is also called a snapdragon; squeeze the flower and the mouth opens). I collected dandelions, pink clover, or any weed that struck my fancy that had a flower or plume. The ones I disliked most were any flowers with tough, hairy stems and sticky sap.

I always thought my dad knew everything because he knew all the plants by name. He took us near marshes where he would cut some cattails for us. They reminded me of hot dogs skewered on a stick. Indians used the down from the mature heads to stuff mattresses.

Dad allowed us to eat bunches of sour grass, also called shamrock. This weed with tiny yellow flowers is better known as wood sorrel. It makes an attractive house plant. Its tiny seed pods explode with only a gentle touch, showering miniscule black seeds in every direction. My neighbor's little children were delighted when they held this plant and felt the pods burst at their slightest touch.

Along the paths, Dad would point out poison sumac and various berries and grasses. Once he plucked some poison ivy and held it in his hand while he showed us how to recognize it by the three leaves—one side of each leaf being noticeably irregular. He warned us never to go near this plant. "Leaves of three, let it be."

One Sunday we went on our usual outing after church, only this time Mom was still dressed in her Sunday best. She wore a brand new white straw cloche hat that day. While hiking across a big field, we came upon a patch of thousands of wild strawberries. We all had to pitch in and pick them.

I lifted the front of my dress and was using it to hold all the berries I gathered. Dad had a few small brown bags to put them in, but we collected more than the bags would hold. Mom was determined to take all of the berries home, so she took off her new white straw hat and filled it with my share of the berries. By the time we got home, her hat was so stained that she could never wear it again, but we had lots of strawberry shortcake all week.

On another trip we picked so many elderberries that they filled several shopping bags. Mom later made jam with the berries. Once we ate wild blackberries right from the bushes, and I can hardly believe that I actually ate all those berries before washing them.

Dad was a veteran and a legionnaire, still it was always his custom to drop a coin into the round container of another American Legion veteran on Memorial Day. For his small donation, he would receive an artificial red poppy. The red poppies that grew wild in Flanders became a memorial symbol to all those who served in France in World War I. John McCrae immortalized them in his poem, "In Flanders Fields."

In the late 1940s when my friends and I were teenagers, we spent many Sunday afternoons at the Conservatory in the Bronx Botanical Garden. We would all get together after Sunday school and spend the day walking in the outdoor gardens and nature paths where trees and bushes were labeled as to natural origin. To see hundreds of lilies displayed in the form of a cross at Easter time was well worth the long bus trip.

My favorite places to visit were and still are the tropical and fern galleries housing lush foliage. Only here could man recreate climactic conditions similar to that of a dense, humid forest. It is like stepping into another part of the world. One can see firsthand many of the rare and unusual plants indigenous to the tropics. There are palm groves, giant ferns, orchids, and insectivorous plants. Visitors can walk through a desert area and see prickly pear cactus, desert flora, and giant saguaro cactus. In spring you will find "lilies of the field"—the anemones—in their own cross-shaped greenhouse.

Some day, take your family or friends on an outing to a garden spot or nursery and stroll among the flowers. You will be amazed at the pleasures in store for you.

The word *garden* has a way of suddenly flooding the mind with thoughts of peace, tranquility, sunny skies, lovely flowers, birds singing, and sparkling fountains.

Jesus often walked in the coolness of the Garden of Gethsemane to be alone to pray and meditate. I cannot help but feel that He loved flowers, and I can picture Him pausing for a moment only to gaze at them and delight in their presence. As He walked along the road, Jesus noticed such things as flowers, trees, and grapevines. This is evidenced in His sermons and parables.

In John 15, Jesus uses the vines and branches metaphorically when explaining our attachment to Him and His attachment to His Father. He tells us that He is the Vine, God the Father is the Gardener, and we are the branches. The gardener removes every branch that does not bear fruit, for it is good for nothing but firewood. The long, wayward branches with sparse leaves and flowers are sapping strength away from the entire plant. Only when they are cut off and the remaining branches are carefully pruned back, will the plant bear richer leaves, blossoms, and abundant fruit at harvest time. The plant becomes healthier, and the pruning enhances its appearance.

Paradoxically, by abiding in Christ and allowing Him to prune and shape our lives, we gain new strength from Him. He also promises that if we abide with Him our joy might be full. Blessed joy! If you do not have the joy of the Lord (John 15:11), you are missing the most precious gift of all, regardless of the wealth of material things you possess.

Jesus often used seeds and gardening as similitudes in parables. In Matthew 13:3–23 He tells of the sower who dropped some seeds (the Word) on the wayside and fowls devoured them (Satan taking away the Word from the hearers' hearts). Some seeds fell on stony ground with little earth. They sprang up and the sun scorched them because they had no roots (at the first sign of persecution these hearers are offended). Some seeds fell among thorns which choked the plants and they yielded no fruit (the lure of the world's lusts took these hearers away). The best seeds were those that fell on good ground and did yield fruit (hearers received the Word and brought forth fruit, thirty, sixty, or a hundredfold). He spoke of faith as small as a grain of mustard seed,

> If ye have faith as a grain of mustard seed, ye shall say unto this mountain, Remove hence to yonder place; and it shall remove; and nothing shall be impossible unto you.
>
> *Matthew 17:20*

When Jesus spoke to the masses, His religious teachings were based on the familiar surroundings and the dilemmas experienced by His listeners. Many of the people crowding around Him were simple farmers who were familiar with problems of sowing and reaping, so they could relate to His stories. His story-telling appealed to them and they understood His manner of speaking in parables.

In His narratives, He used regional subjects like tares and wheat (Matthew 13:24–30), laborers in the vineyard (Matthew

45

20:1–16) and the barren fig tree (Luke 13:6–9) as allegories. The people marvelled when Jesus compared fruit-bearing trees (Matthew 7:17–20) to believers bringing forth fruit. These stories were simply told, but contained profound messages that led to self-examination then and still do today. Jesus used a tree in the following verse to illustrate the remarkable power of faith:

> And the Lord said, If ye had faith as a grain of mustard seed, ye might say unto this sycamine tree, Be thou plucked up by the root, and be thou planted in the sea; and it should obey you.
>
> *Luke 17:6*

I had been talking about trees earlier; they are God's beautiful and very useful gifts that must not be taken for granted.

> Out of the ground made the Lord God to grow every tree that is pleasant to the sight, and good for food.
>
> *Genesis 2:9*

How often do we value a tree in our yard because it is so pleasant to look upon and to sit beneath? Some people travel long distances to see and photograph the lofty wonders like the sequoia trees in California. These towering giants of the plant world live to be 3,000 years old. One reaches a height of over 260 feet tall and 40 feet wide, with roots covering more than 3 acres. Their longevity is attributed to the fact that they have bark up to two feet thick containing tannin, which protects it from insect attack.

Tourists by the thousands flock to Washington, D.C., in the spring to view the cherry blossoms in bloom. There they can witness a scene of resurrected beauty once every year. Cherry trees are just some of the natural beauties God placed on earth for us to enjoy.

Another sightseeing attraction is the Hudson River Valley in New York at apple blossom time. The landscape is alive with glorious pastel flowers covering the trees, and their fragrance permeates the air. Did you know that the branches are very short and strong so that the apples will not knock against each other when the wind blows? This is one of the ways God protects the fruit from being bruised.

Peach blossoms decorate the orchards for a short time with acres and acres of lacy delicate hues.

> Who looks with love upon the flower
> Will contemplate the root;
> Nor can he well forget the tree
> Who relishes the fruit.
> Dull-hued indeed am I, the flower,
> If faith, the root, be dry;
> But nourished with the precious blood,
> The fruit is Christ, not I.
>
> *Sister Miriam, "The Root of Jesse"*[16]

Mankind with its sophisticated knowledge and brilliant God-given intellect can find its way to the moon and back, but can it create anything comparable to the awesome beauty and majesty of a tree in bloom?

The flowers and stamens on the fruit trees play an important part in the process of reproduction. After they have completed their fertilization function, they wither and fall off, leaving the ovaries containing seeds to swell and ripen into fruit. First the showy flowers, then the fruit. Not only did the Lord God create the trees to bear fruit for our eating pleasure, but He made them pleasant to look upon by dressing them in a grand and stately manner.

Two thousand years ago, one tree had a very sad task to perform in a place called *Calvary.*

There is an analogy between the Spirit-filled believer and fruit-bearing trees in the following verses. Some contain explicit promises of prosperity for the believer.

> And he shall be like a tree planted by the rivers of water, that bringeth forth his fruit in his season; his leaf also shall not wither; and whatsoever he doeth shall prosper.
>
> *Psalm 1:3*

Blessed is the man who trusts in the Lord, whose confidence is in him. He will be like a tree planted by the water that sends out its roots by the stream. It does not fear when heat comes; its leaves are always green. It has no worries in a year of drought and never fails to bear fruit.

Jeremiah 17:7, 8 NIV

In the next verse, the believer is compared to a garden. Abundant life is promised to those who trust in God.

And the Lord shall guide thee continually, and satisfy thy soul in drought, and make fat thy bones: and thou shalt be like a watered garden, and like a spring of water, whose waters fail not.

Isaiah 58:11

However, to those who trust not in God,

He will be like a bush in the wastelands; he will not see prosperity when it comes. He will dwell in the parched places of the desert, in a salt land where no one lives.

Jeremiah 17:6 NIV

Gardens were frequently mentioned in the Bible. It is interesting to know that God put the first man and the first garden together. What a beautiful setting He chose for man's first home.

And the Lord God planted a garden eastward in Eden; and there he put the man whom he had formed.

Genesis 2:8

And a river went out of Eden to water the garden.

Genesis 2:10

God placed the man in the Garden of Eden as its gardener, to tend and care for it.

Genesis 2:15 LB

Here was a place where Adam would have some pleasant work to do and a place where his food would be provided. God planted many trees from which Adam and Eve could freely eat, but He also placed one tree of which they were forbidden to eat. Because they ate the fruit from this tree—the tree of the knowledge of good and evil—God sent them from the Garden of Eden forever and cursed the ground so that it would bring forth thorns and thistles, sorrow and toil. From that moment when the man and woman were banished from the garden to till the ground by the sweat of their brow, agriculture became the most important and necessary industry.

In Genesis 4:2 we read that Cain was a tiller of the ground. Further on, in Genesis 9:20, Noah planted a vineyard, and in Joseph's time, Egypt yielded corn as the sand of the sea, Genesis 41:49. Gideon was threshing wheat when God called him, Judges 6:11. In Ruth, Chapter 2, we learn that Ruth gleaned corn, barley, and wheat in the fields after the harvesters. During their wanderings in the wilderness with Moses, the Israelites spoke of the cucumbers, melons, leeks, onions, and garlic that they ate when they were in Egypt (Numbers 11:5). Besides planting vineyards, olive groves, orchards, fig trees, pomegranates, and dates, the Israelites cultivated crops of lentils, flax, and grains. They tended gardens for use as cool, private places where they could retire to walk, talk, meditate, and sometimes bathe. The gardens and vineyards were often surrounded by hedges or walls to protect the crops from destructive animals and thieves. A small booth may have stood at one corner to house a watchman.

Gardens also served as burial sites. When Abraham's wife, Sarah, died, Abraham purchased a field in Machpelah from Ephron the Hittite for 400 shekels of silver. It was located near Mamre in the land of Canaan, and a large garden surrounded by trees was situated at the end of the field. In the garden was the cave that Abraham used as a sepulchre for Sarah. Later Abraham was buried there by his sons, Isaac and Ishmael. Eventually, Isaac, Jacob, and their wives, Rebecca and Leah, were also buried in the cave of Machpelah.

A new garden tomb owned by Joseph of Arimathea became the temporary burial place from which Jesus triumphantly arose after three days.

Now in the place where he was crucified there was a garden; and in the garden a new sepulchre, wherein was never man yet laid. There laid they Jesus.

John 19:41, 42

To
everything
there is
a season

N ot only are plants adapted to grow in a particular geo-
graphical zone, but there is also a time for everything
under the heaven.

There are spring plantings and fall plantings; early bloomers
and late bloomers; winter, spring, summer, and fall flowers.

In my own front yard, the perennial crocuses with their
grasslike leaves are the vanguard of spring. While the snow yet
covers the lawns, these tubular flowers are the first to arrive. They
are followed by daffodils and tulips; yellow flowering forsythia
bushes; and white, pink, and red azaleas. Later in the spring,
dogwood and lilacs bloom. All summer there are marigolds,
impatiens, petunias, and a host of annuals and perennials. At the
end of the summer and as late as November, sometimes in the
snow, the chrysanthemums are blooming. Two popular indoor
flowering plants at Christmas time are the poinsettia and the
Christmas cactus.

Each plant has its own short growing season in which it
matures, flowers, and bears fruit. Our lives follow a similar course:
"As for man, his days are as grass: as a flower of the field, so he

flourisheth" (Psalm 103:15). God sets us in a certain place at a particular time because there is someone there who needs your help at that precise time. Similarly, plants are rooted and grounded in the soil and cannot go anywhere, but they must remain in the very spot where they were planted. They absorb moisture from the air through their leaves and from the soil through their roots. The moisture penetrates and feeds every cell within their system. When they have reached the peak of their growth, they produce the fruit for which they were sown.

You have been planted in your little spot, but unlike the plant which must stay put once rooted, God gave you the power to move about. If you do not like the "climate," you do not have to remain in the place where you were "planted." Perhaps you may best serve Him on the other side of town or the other side of the world.

If you are uncertain how you may best serve Him; if you feel your life is empty, fruitless, unfulfilled, and devoid of meaning, then remain "rooted" and allow the presence of Christ to permeate every fiber of your being. How? By reading His Word, praying, and listening. As the flower seeks the sun for life and sustenance, so must you also seek the Son for life. Bask in His presence, and you will grow in grace, knowledge, and understanding. If you seek wisdom from the Lord, then Proverbs, Chapter 2, can be a source of guidance. In due season, the very purpose for your existence will be revealed to you. You will become a useful vessel and produce the "fruit" for which you were "sown."

God did not create you to be a nobody. He created you and everything else for a purpose. Rev. Charles H. Spurgeon stated it like this: "There is not a single insect fluttering in the breeze but accomplisheth some divine decree; and I will never have it that God created any man, especially any Christian man, to be a blank, and to be a nothing. He made you for an end. Find out what that end is; find out your niche, and fill it. If it be ever so little, if it is only to be a hewer of wood and drawer of water, do something in this great battle for God and truth."[17]

What can you do that is better than leading someone to Christ, and what better time is there to start than right now? To the unsaved, the Bible warns, "Behold, now is the accepted time; behold, now is the day of salvation" (II Corinthians 6:2). Someone once phrased the entire message so meaningfully in only two little lines: "Only one life, 'twill soon be past. Only what's done for Christ will last."[18] We all have a given amount of time, and what we do for Christ in that allotted time is the only thing that counts.

> For all flesh is as grass, and all the glory of man as the flower of grass. The grass withereth, and the flower thereof falleth away: But the word of the Lord endureth for ever.
>
> *I Peter 1:24–25*

Listen to the following dynamic words by Rev. Spurgeon:

> Sleepy Christian, let me shout in thine ears: thou art sleeping while souls are being lost, sleeping while men are being damned, sleeping while hell is being peopled, sleeping while Christ is being dishonored, sleeping while the devil is grinning at thy sleepy face, sleeping while demons are dancing around thy slumbering carcass, and telling it in hell that a Christian is asleep. You will never catch the devil asleep; let not the devil catch you asleep. Watch, and be sober, that ye may be always up to your duty.[19]

What a powerful message! The devil will never miss a chance to catch us off guard, with our defenses down. He looks for an opening in the hedge (Job 1:10), hoping to find a way to defeat us. One of his wily tactics is to drive fear and confusion into those who love the Lord. In his own cunning way, this evil one will attempt to sow discord among family members, friends, and even church members.

> Be sober, be vigilant; because your adversary the devil, as a roaring lion, walketh about, seeking whom he may devour.
>
> *I Peter 5:8*

One way to send Satan running is to pray without ceasing and keep on praising the Lord, even in the midst of trying circumstances.

In your own way, where you are, you can do something for the Lord. He can use you because "the harvest truly is plenteous, but the laborers are few" (Matthew 9:37). The born-again believer must never let an opportunity slip by to win souls into the Kingdom. Perhaps we may never pass their way again. As a result, they may never get to hear the Gospel message, and may be lost forever.

> If thou shalt confess with thy mouth the Lord Jesus, and shalt believe in thine heart that God hath raised Him from the dead, thou shalt be saved.
>
> *Romans 10:9*

Before leaving my home to attend "Word of Life" radio broadcast rallies years ago, I always asked my parents to be sure to listen to the program on the radio that same evening, and they did listen. Even though I had accepted Christ and my parents brought us up to believe in God, we never talked about salvation or being "born again." I can only hope that my father responded when the invitation was given at the end of the programs, because when he died accidentally a few years later, I never knew whether he was saved. I will not know until I see him in Glory. I had many an opportunity to witness to my father, but I let them go for another time. That "other time" never came.

The only thing you can take to Heaven with you are the people whom Jesus redeemed because *you* took the time to witness and they, in turn, believed the Gospel truth.

Shakespeare penned the words, "When I consider everything that grows holds in perfection but a little moment."[20] This may very well be your little moment of perfection, your time to praise, your time to serve. Do not let it pass you by. Reach out your hand. There is someone waiting for your help this very day. If you wait much longer, it may be too late.

For what is your life? It is even a vapor that appeareth for a little time, and then vanisheth away.

James 4:14

He that winneth souls is wise.

Proverbs 11:30

He hath
made
everything
beautiful

In a previous chapter I mentioned how some plants adapt to survive extreme hot or cold environmental temperatures. But there are other plants that need full sun, plants that thrive better in the shade, some that need lots of water, some that need little water, some that climb as vines, and some that hug the ground.

Similarly, not all people can tolerate living in the same climate. Some can tolerate living in cold areas, some adapt better to the heat. There are folks who love to sit for hours on the beach, and there are others who must sit under a shady tree.

If it were not for the fact that some folks can work long hours in the hot sun, we would not have farmers and people to pick crops. Others, who do not mind the cold, work better in the freezing weather and snow. We depend on them in the city to work outdoors, installing and repairing electrical and telephone wires and gas and water pipes. There are some who work underground all day in subways and mines. It takes a special kind of person to handle that sort of work.

Others build skyscrapers. It is astonishing to see those workers miles up in the air with nothing but a steel beam under them.

They walk along those narrow beams as though it were a broad way. Surely, they deserve our applause, as do the window washers on high-rise buildings.

Without scientists and explorers who have the training and the stamina to endure extreme weather conditions, we would have no knowledge of what goes on in the remote parts of the world. We would not be aware of the vegetation and flowers in the deserts and arctics if someone did not go there to research.

God gave each person the extraordinary gift of being able to accomplish something that someone else could not do, under conditions that would cause another person great physical hardship.

The fact that we all prefer a different climate is, in itself, a miracle, otherwise we would all be living together, crowded in one place on earth where the temperature would not vary too much.

Even though we do not all enjoy the same environment, we depend on one another tremendously. We need our families, neighbors, employers, and employees as well as builders, farmers, pastors, teachers, shop keepers, and police officers. We all play a different role, each contributing to the welfare of others.

Whether you believe it or not, you have a special characteristic about you that is quite different from everyone else, making you a unique being. You are needed because somebody depends on you to do for them what they cannot do for themselves.

God wants you to do something useful *now,* never mind how insignificant it may seem. Perhaps your purpose is to help (with a cheerful spirit) an aging parent to manage physically and financially. Perhaps a neighbor who does not have an automobile needs a lift to the supermarket and back. Your small children need to be taught honesty; fair play; love of their fellow human beings, country, and God, and only you can instill these values in them while they are young.

Maybe you can go on a shopping errand for a sick friend, or take some flowers. There are so many ways to bring pleasure and ease the burdens of another. Gifts that come from the heart have more value and need not be costly. Send a card, bake a cake, or give a small trinket with meaning. Listen to their woes and bear their burdens. Be the good Samaritan. Do it all in the name of Jesus, for He said,

> Inasmuch as ye have done it unto one of the least of these my brethren, ye have done it unto me.
>
> *Matthew 25:40*

If you take the initiative, you can think of a lot of ways to help others. In so doing, you are enriching your own life more than you know, and you really are serving God when you reach out in love. For this very purpose you were created. Remember, no matter how bad things seem to be for you, there is always somebody who is far worse off than you are.

You may have a parent in a distant city you have not been in touch with for some time. He or she may have a need you know nothing about and at this moment is asking God for help. If you write a note and enclose a check, you are being used of God to answer that prayer. You have no way of knowing how many prayers are answered by your kindness to others.

A gift need not be an elaborate expensive item. Sometimes the smallest token can mean the most to a person. A book on your shelf or even a book mark can convey a message of great thoughtfulness.

Giving to one another as well as to the Lord's work is an important and necessary part of the Christian walk, whether in the form of tithing, giving of your services, your time, or all of these combined.

> Every man according as he purposeth in his heart, so let him give; not grudgingly, or of necessity; for God loveth a cheerful giver.
>
> *II Corinthians 9:7*

Anonymous giving is most rewarding, for it embraces the true spirit of sharing, one in which you ask nothing in return. God knows the secrets of the heart and He rewards accordingly (II Corinthians 9:8).

You can never outgive God, for when you give, it will be given back to you, good measure, pressed down, and running over (Luke 6:38). Paul also explains that God will remember our giving. He will apply it to our account and return it to us with interest.

> Not because I desire a gift: but I desire fruit that may abound to your account.
>
> *Philippians 4:17*

The Word promises that tithes and offerings are multiplied back.

> Bring ye all the tithes into the storehouse, that there may be meat in mine house, and prove me now herewith, saith the Lord of hosts, if I will not open you the windows of heaven, and pour you out a blessing, that there shall not be room enough to receive it.
>
> *Malachi 3:10*

From my own experience I can honestly say that the principle of giving and receiving does work in the most remarkable, unexpected way. The ministries that I give to are not getting rich on my small donations, but *I* am! The little seed I sow always produces a harvest. If you plant, you can expect to gather. It's God's unchanging law.

> While the earth remaineth, seedtime and harvest ... shall not cease.
>
> *Genesis 8:22*

The following little verse is a constant reminder that God always provides:

> "What, giving again?" I asked in dismay.
> "And must I keep giving and giving away?"

"Oh, no," said the angel, piercing me through,
"Just give till the Father stops giving to you."

Anonymous, "What, Giving Again?"[21]

Many years ago I attended a service at Calvary Baptist Church in New York City. The speaker that week was a well-known pastor from Grand Rapids, Michigan, and I did want to see and hear him in person. That same night, my friends and I each purchased one of his books, and after the service he graciously offered to sign them. That particular book, *Broken Things* by the late Dr. M.R. DeHaan, meant a great deal to me. Some years later when I learned that my brother was studying to go into the ministry, I gave him my favorite book, knowing he would find it very helpful. This is part of the thank-you letter I received from my brother, who is now the pastor of a Methodist church in Alabama:

I especially felt that I should write you today to tell you about the book, *Broken Things,* that you gave me. In between my studies and my text books, I finally got the chance to read it. It is a most marvelous book of inspired lessons and I will never be able to thank you enough for it. Many of the chapters in it were reflections of many things I have thought and felt, and it really touched me very deeply to see someone else express exactly the same feelings as I have had.

I especially wanted to let you know that I not only feel a very close, personal relationship to the concepts expressed, but I will use it as a basis of many sermons, public and private, as I go through the ministry.

I will always treasure this little book and preach from it and will especially treasure the thought that it came from you. I find that God works endlessly in so many subtle ways. Although we are sister and brother, time, distance, and life have separated us in so many ways, yet your kind gesture I feel is an outward sign purposed by God to let us know that love and understanding in so many ways will never grow separated. Thank you again, dear sister, for you could have searched long and hard and expensively, but never found a more appropriate and welcome gift.[22]

Would you like to receive such a letter in response to some small gesture on your part? The book may have blessed him, but his letter touched me even more. Little did I realize how much the book would mean to him when I slipped it into his hand as he was about to board a plane. This taught me that, not only should I give, but when I receive, I should acknowledge the gift with very warm words of appreciation to let that person know how grateful I really am.

During the writing of this book, some of my friends have given me small gifts that brought me such great joy. One friend gave me a perfumed bookmark with a picture of a jasmine on it, because she knew I was doing some research on flowers from which perfumes are made. Another friend sent note paper with pictures of pansies, for she knew they were fast becoming my favorite flower. One morning, a neighbor left a package on my doorstep containing a lovely hardcover book on flowers. Another friend gave me a scented artificial rose on a stickpin. During the summer, one lady brought me a single magnificent rose from her garden with a good-luck note and left it on my desk at work. A small gift with meaning is a treasured gift.

Be a blessing to somebody before another day passes. God wants to use you. Let Him. You may never know how much your kind act will lift the spirit of a friend in need of comfort. It is just another way of planting seeds, from which you will reap your harvest—hundredfold, sixtyfold, or thirtyfold.

If you have a dried, pressed flower tucked away in the pages of a book, it probably stirs up vivid recollections of some cherished moment in your past. It also brings with it a remembrance of the special person involved. It must have been a pleasant occasion, or you would not have preserved a memento to remind you of it forever.

So it is with everyone whose life we touch, even for a passing moment. The memory is indelibly imprinted in the mind, and images are etched in the heart. How wonderful if we could leave every person we meet with the memory of a pleasant thought to be smiled upon later or an act worthy of remembering in some future time.

A courteous bus driver who waits a few moments extra for you and greets you with a smile can certainly make your day a lot brighter. In return, your warm and friendly greeting can do a lot to cheer the driver who may have had a frustrating day.

We can take some advice from the bee. As it visits each flower, it is busy gathering honey to take back to its honeycomb. We ought to gather some honey along the way from everyone with whom we associate, even a stranger stopping to ask directions.

Pleasant words are as an honeycomb, sweet to the soul, and health to the bones.

Proverbs 16:24

Usually, I tend to shy away from strangers. Almost every day on the crowded city streets there are people handing out leaflets to passers-by. Normally I would go around the person or put my hands in my pockets, hoping to avoid taking the handbill, because there are so many of them. One ends up holding five or six papers and has to carry them to the nearest litter basket. Only recently I made it my business to go right up to the person, take the paper, smile, and say: "Thank you, God loves you and so do I." I have to admit the first time I tried this, I startled myself, but the result was so positive that I do it all the time now. The person grinned from ear to ear and said, "Lady, I love you too, thank you." Other people have responded with "God bless you," with a surprised smile, or with "Have a good day." I know the joy we shared for that split second is just a little drop of honey to take back to the honeycomb.

If you want to see a face light up with thanks, try rushing to open a door for the person delivering a load of packages. It is not easy trying to open a door with elbows and feet while both arms are holding clumsy bundles.

He has made everything beautiful in its time. . . . I know that there is nothing better for men than to be happy and do good while they live.

Ecclesiastes 3:11, 12 NIV

Let us not be weary in well doing: for in due season we shall reap, if we faint not.

Galatians 6:9

Am I my brother's keeper?

There may be some valuable lessons to be gleaned from every situation we find ourselves involved in. From early childhood when we touched something hot for the first time, we learned the hard way that it burns and that we must not do it again. All through life we come up against affairs of the heart—separation from loved ones, financial loss, mental and physical problems. However, no matter how bad it seems at the time, no experience is ever wasted.

What we learn from our most profound experiences will either help us avoid the same mistakes the next time around; teach us patience, fortitude, and dependence on God; or give us the opportunity to pass on the knowledge we have acquired to someone else facing the same kind of problem.

In raising our children, we frequently have to give them advice based on our own experience. Often this influences and encourages them. But sometimes our advice goes unheeded, and they in turn have to learn through their own trial and error.

History books are documented with facts that are studied by experts when mapping out war strategy and military operations. Today's experts need to learn as much as possible from past experiences in order to prevent the same mistakes from recurring. Such important information can be extremely beneficial in planning current maneuvers.

You are not living solely unto yourself. Even though you may be completely unaware of the fact, your life, in some way, is intermingled and interwoven with the lives of all those with whom your path crosses. John Donne expressed this thought as follows:

> No man is an island, entire of itself; every man is a piece of the continent, a part of the main; if a clod be washed away by the sea, Europe is the less, as well as if a promontory were, as well as if a manor of thy friends or of thine own were; any man's death diminishes me, because I am involved in mankind; and therefore never send to know for whom the bell tolls; it tolls for thee.
>
> *John Donne, "No Man Is an Island"*[23]

True, we are all in one way or another involved in mankind. We are all in this together. We need one another just as plants need other plants for the purpose of cross-pollinating. Imagine what would happen to bird life in the desert if there were no cacti? At least half of the bird population would disappear. What would become of the cactus if there were no birds to disperse the seeds? Wildlife and botanical life depend on each other for survival. Insects, plants, and animals need one another to create a balance in the ecosystem. Likewise, people need other people in order to survive. Sometimes we have to take a supportive stand by organizing unions to back up one another when there are grievances at work. Men and women from all walks of life, in colleges, religious organizations, business, and medicine, unite together when debating the pros and cons of every important issue concerning life. There is strength in unity.

Every person is endowed with many natural God-given talents. Some are artistic, some fantastic with figures, some know how to earn money, some to teach, some to cook, and some have a flair for public speaking. Others have a way with children, a way with plants, and a way with animals. There are good soldiers, good doctors, good preachers, and good musicians. If I have left you out, it is only because the list would be endless. You have something very special to offer in the very place where you are now. If you have not yet discovered what it is, then be assured that the potential is there. You do have something very worthwhile to contribute in your lifetime. You can make someone else's life a little better just by having known you.

God created every person, every flower, every creature, and loves every person equally, so what can we do when faced with people with whom we find it very difficult to get along, much less love? There are people in our daily encounters, at work, next door, living above us, or even in our own family who make life most unpleasant and cause great bitterness. Unfortunately, there are no guidebooks from which to draw instant answers. We need all the help we can get, and the only thing to do at times like these is turn to the Lord in prayer and to search the Scriptures. The problem may not get solved overnight, but He will help see us through. It is possible that the problem is the very thing that keeps us humble and is God's way of showing how much we need to depend on Him.

> I want you to trust me in your times of trouble, so I can rescue you, and you can give me glory.
>
> *Psalm 50:14, 15 LB*

The following is a case in point illustrating how one person's life affects another's. I have two dear friends who are sisters, living in a lovely apartment building for many years. Their home is attractive, and they live quietly; one is retired, and one still goes to business. These women have many friends in their building. They enjoy the neighborhood—their church, transportation systems, many shops, the library, and parks are all within walking distance. It sounds so ideal, and it was, until a young family moved over them and turned their life upside down.

Long into the night they suffered loss of sleep from the loud stereo and television above them. There were noisy parties weekdays and weekends lasting until the small hours. My friend went to work tired and upset, and her sister often could not enjoy one of her few pleasures, her own radio and television, during the day because of the loud noise overhead. An attempt to speak gently to the offending couple about the noise proved futile.

After months and months of anxiety and suffering, they were forced to seek an attorney and take civil action. The sisters are both Christians, and the last thing they desire is to cause further problems involving lawsuits. It goes against everything they ever believed in. Their action led to retaliatory threats from the tenants overhead, and for a while they had real reason to fear.

What good has come from this experience? For one thing, as close as they were to the Lord before, they have drawn much closer to Him now. By getting together with little groups of neighbors in their building, they are holding prayer meetings and Bible study classes. They have reached out to pray for others in need, and their faith has been tried, tested, and proven strong. They firmly believed God would have a lesson for them in this situation, and they trusted Him for an answer. The problem was eventually resolved through peaceable means.

You can divulge your feelings of bitterness to the Lord and storm the gates of Heaven with complaints about your neighbor, but do not expect God to take your part against any person, for "God is no respecter of persons" (Acts 10:34) and "He maketh his sun to rise on the evil and on the good, and sendeth rain on the just and on the unjust" (Matthew 5:45). He also makes the sun to shine on the weeds as well as the flowers and the rain to fall on the good seeds as well as the bad seeds at the same time, so that both the weeds and flowers grow together in the same patch of ground, and the wheat and tares grow in the same field.

Your only alternative is to pray for those who despitefully use you and persecute you and say all manner of evil against you. Hard as it may be to understand, this is a lesson in discipleship. Jesus loved and forgave those who hurt him.

By this shall all men know that ye are my disciples, if ye have love one to another.

John 13:35

A rose is so beautiful, yet it has thorns that prick our fingers. We still love roses in spite of thorns, which incidentally, were put there in the first place for a good reason. By comparison, the ones we love often cause us pain. Sometimes praying for the person who gives you the most trouble may lead to an unexpected change in the relationship. In a quarrelsome situation, only the wisdom of Solomon can help.

A soft answer turneth away wrath; but grievous words stir up anger.

Proverbs 15:1

It is so important to cultivate friendships, because more than anything we need friends. A good friend is one with whom we can share spiritual matters, who encourages and uplifts when we are feeling discouraged.

A man that hath friends must show himself friendly: and there is a friend that sticketh closer than a brother.

Proverbs 18:24

God has blessed me with good friends and neighbors, but I have special friends with whom there is an invisible bond of unity. I can discuss the Father's business with them and each of them are like precious links in a golden chain. Whatever our needs be, we can unashamedly ask one another to pray about them. In Paul's words, we are "mutually encouraged by each other's faith" (Romans 1:12 NIV). King Saul's son, Jonathan, searched tirelessly for his beloved friend, David, until he found him just to encourage him and strengthen him in his faith (I Samuel 23:16). That is the greatest gift we can give one another. How, then, can

I be my brother's keeper? "Bear ye one another's burdens, and so fulfill the law of Christ" (Galatians 6:2).

The following verse is a kind tribute to friendship:

When troubles come your soul to try,
You love a friend who just stands by:
Perhaps there's nothing he can do,
The thing is strictly up to you.
For there are troubles all your own,
And paths the soul must tread alone,
Bad times when love can't smooth the road,
Nor friendship lift the heavy load.
But just to feel you have a friend,
Who will stand by until the end,
Whose sympathy through all endures,
Whose warm handclasp is always yours,
It helps somehow to pull you through,
Although there's nothing he can do.
And so with fervent heart we cry:
"God bless the friend who just stands by."

Anonymous, "Friends"[24]

How true! Sometimes even your best friend cannot help, but there is one Friend who can lift the heavy load, one Friend who will walk the path with you, one Friend who has everything under control. He is the *only* One you can count on. He will be the best Friend you ever had. Jesus said it Himself:

Ye are my friends.

John 15:14

Let your light shine

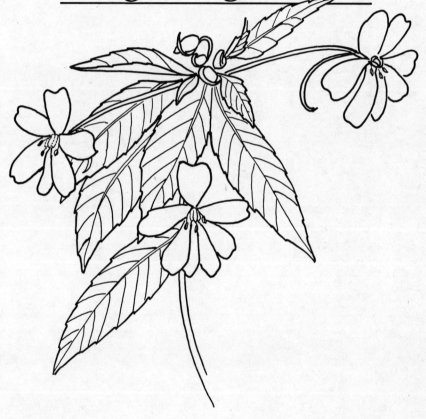

Beautiful cultivated gardens and attractive, well-kept lawns are never just happenstance. The trim, weed-free results you see are the work of concerned gardeners who diligently labor over them with loving care and constant attention. The gardeners trim, prune, remove dead growth, water, and feed the plants attentively. They will not permit troublesome weeds and crabgrass to grow in their lovely gardens, nor spoil the even texture of their lawns. They know that if unchecked, the ubiquitous plants will grow rampant. Their roots will spread deep and strong, robbing the soil of valuable nutrients, choking and crowding the smaller desirable plants to the extent of disfiguring and stunting their growth. Despite removal, weeds continue to grow because their seeds remain in the soil. As often as they keep returning, the pernicious weeds must be plucked out before they have a chance to establish a firm foothold. The longer they stay in the garden, the harder it is to remove them and the more destructive they become.

Weeds growing in a garden are not unlike problems that invade our thoughts from time to time. What can we do about the fears, frustrations, and uncertainties that creep into our thoughts now and then? No one is immune to these feelings. Fear does arise, anxiety does rear its ugly head, discouragement does creep in, and doubts do take root, crowding and choking our ability to think clearly at times. These are the "weeds of trepidation" that need to be rooted out. We cannot prevent negative feelings from arising within us any more than we can stop unwelcome picture images from parading through our heads. After all, we are human and susceptible to every kind of human emotion. What we must try to do is prevent anxiety from overwhelming our thoughts to the exclusion of all others, thus robbing our peace of mind. Distressing thoughts must be plucked out or "nipped in the bud" before they develop the same tenacity as the rambunctious weed.

The time spent brooding over problems wastes precious moments that could be better spent in quiet communion with God. The only way I know—until someone comes up with a better way—of handling anxiety and discouragement is by persistent prayer—morning, noon, and evening prayer. God is the Gardener who will remove the "weeds of despair" growing in our garden.

When we as Christians experience anxiety, doubt, and worry, we suffer twofold—first, from the cause of the problem; and second, from a sense of guilt and shame to think that we dared to allow fear and worry to enter our mind in the first place. One day we earnestly committed our lives to God and promised that we would always trust Him. Therefore, we reason, if anything can upset us that much, then we are simply not trusting Him enough. We struggle for perfection and suffer when we do not measure up to the standards that constitute Christian living. We forget that we are human, and can never, ever be perfect.

Each day we pray, "Today I will follow Christ's example and try to be like Him," and each night we confess, "Father, forgive me for I have fallen short again and committed the same old sins." How often have you prayed that same prayer? In all sincerity we keep on promising God and ourselves that we are going to do better next time. There is nothing wrong with that. Keep on striving to do good, and as often as you fail, ask the Lord to forgive you (He will, dear friend), and then start over. Basically, we know to do good; to be unselfish, thoughtful, and generous, yet we do not always live up to our good intentions the way we had hoped. The strife between the desire to do good and actually doing it is a never-ending battle.

Paul had to fight this same battle between the two natures. He knew what he "ought" to do, yet he behaved quite the opposite. Said Paul,

I do not understand what I do.
For what I want to do I do not do,
but what I hate I do.
And if I do what I do not want to do,
I agree that the law is good.
As it is, it is no longer I myself who do it,
but it is sin living in me.
I know that nothing good lives in me,
that is, in my sinful nature.
For I have the desire to do what is good,
but I cannot carry it out.
For what I do is not the good I want to do;
no, the evil I do not want to do—this I keep on doing.
Now if I do what I do not want to do,
it is no longer I who do it,
but it is sin living in me that does it.
So I find this law at work:
When I want to do good, evil is right there with me.

Romans 7:15–21 NIV

Paul continues, "What a wretched man I am!" (Romans 7:24 NIV). In his mind he served God's law, but with the flesh, the law of sin (Romans 7:25). By sheer perseverance and dependence on God for support, Paul was victorious in his great battle for the Lord, because in the end he was able to say,

I have fought a good fight, I have finished my course, I have kept the faith: Henceforth there is laid up for me a crown of righteousness.

II Timothy 4:7

In other words, Paul remained faithful to God.

How I yearn to live an exemplary Christian life, a devout life. Would that I could, but how weak and human I am, slipping and falling day after day, continually calling on the Lord to help me to do better, to pick me up when I fall. Since the Bible gives me all the instructions, I am well aware of my role as a child of God—forgive seventy times seven, love my enemies, be slow to anger, bridle the tongue, give to him that asketh, pray for them that persecute, trust God, fear not, have faith, and follow the Ten Commandments. However, in spite of my good intentions, I break the rules every day, not deliberately, but by omission. My own personal feelings are expressed in the text paraphrased in the Living Bible.

> It seems to be a fact of life that when I want to do what is right, I inevitably do what is wrong, . . . but there is something else deep within me, in my lower nature, that is at war with my mind and wins the fight and makes me a slave to the sin that is still within me. . . . Oh, what a terrible predicament I'm in.

Romans 7:21, 24 LB

I know that I am not to give way to anxiety and depression, nor am I to withhold good when it is in the power of my hand to do it (Proverbs 3:27), yet I, too, inevitably fall short of the mark.

How often we do the very things we promise ourselves we will *not* do, and forget to do the things we say we *will* do, though we have a strong desire to do them? It happens to me daily. On the one hand (my spiritual nature at work), I find myself praising God many times during the day and thanking Him for "things" that He gives me—a friend's thoughtful gesture, a new dress, a pleasant encounter, a nice day, food, health, home, and family. I remember also to give compliments and words of praise to another. More often than not, I find myself falling asleep while counting my blessings. On the other hand (my human nature at work), there are many times when I withhold that well-deserved compliment, or I am too quick to find fault. I become too impatient, frustrated, and aggravated over some insignificant event that occurred during the day—missing a bus and waiting in the cold for a half hour, or waiting on slow-moving lines at the super-market checkout or the bank. Other sources of irritation may be a broken promise of something I was looking forward to, some unpleasant appointment I must face, or an especially unkind remark aimed my way. All of these are of such minor importance, yet they tend to grow all out of proportion, getting the best of me, causing anxious moments and perhaps even a sleepless night. How difficult to live a Spirit-filled, care-free existence when one is blindly groping with all sorts of petty annoyances and meaningless trivia.

It is so easy to live the desired victorious life when alone in a room or with people who share our faith, for it seems that the Holy Spirit dwells in that realm with us. That quiet time of devotion one shares with God can be rewarding and enriching. Anyone spending hours searching the Scriptures and talking with God certainly will be spiritually blessed and the hungry will be filled. It would be ideal to escape to blissful solitude, away from the cares and problems of the day, but life is not like that, and we cannot always reside in such an environment. We have to live right where the action is, in the midst of dissension on the job, with our neighbors, and even our own families. We get involved in problems that are often not even of our own choosing, and we cannot escape our participation in these encounters because our lives are so closely woven and meshed together. These are the "weeds of discord" that spring up and spoil the harmony of the flowerbed.

It certainly does get discouraging at times, and there are days when it seems that we stand alone against the world. We have to go about our daily business in a world among people of different faiths. Try as we may, we cannot please everyone. Not everyone appreciates us, and not everyone thinks or believes the way we do, and not everyone understands us. Our priorities are not the same as the world's. Folks wonder how we can have a good time going to a prayer breakfast or attending a crusade meeting. We would rather read Christian literature and the Bible than the latest best-selling novel, and we would rather see a Christian TV program than the latest movie or Broadway show.

Perhaps it would be so much easier to conform to the things of the world and keep our faith to ourselves. By keeping quiet we won't make waves and be subject to ridicule, nor will we give the impression that there is something a little different about us. No, we must take a firm stand for the Lord's sake and dare to be different from the crowd. Jesus was very explicit when He said, "He that is not with me is against me" (Matthew 12:30). There is no middle ground, no compromise, no fence-sitting.

Jeremiah the prophet knew what it meant to stand alone before the crowd. In a vision God said to him, "You are to go to Jerusalem as my spokesman, to tell the people what I will command you to say." Jeremiah went reluctantly and as a result, he was ridiculed for his preaching. He cried out to God, "What am I to do Lord? See how I have been made a laughing stock because I obeyed you? If I continue this way, I will be scorned, yet I do not wish to stop serving you." God said, "Do not talk foolishly; Trust Me and I will deliver you from the hand of your enemies. You will be to them as solid as a stone wall." I like the words that God spoke to Jeremiah, "You are to influence them, not let them influence you" (Jeremiah 15:19 LB). In the New Testament, Jesus gave the following command to all who would be His disciples:

Ye are the light of the world. . . . Neither do men light a candle, and put it under a bushel, but on a candlestick; and it giveth light unto all that are in the house. Let your light so shine before men, that they may see your good works, and glorify your Father which is in Heaven.

Matthew 5:14–16

That sounds like a direct order not to hide our relationship with Jesus under a bushel basket nor be ashamed to speak of Him in daily conversation, but let it be known that He reigns supreme in our lives. By doing so, we are giving Him glory. I have known people to scoff at the mention of Jesus, and it is almost a personal affront to me. It hurts me when they do so. His name is far from their heart, but always on their lips vainly being used as an exclamation, or worse.

> ... sanctify the Lord God in your hearts: and be ready always to give an answer to every man that asketh you a reason of the hope that is in you.
>
> *I Peter 3:15*

Be ready and willing to talk openly about the Jesus you know, the One to whom your life is entrusted. This can be done gently, in a Spirit of love, without being overbearing or forceful.

I wear a "Jesus First" lapel pin all the time. These two little words are by no means subtle; they come right out with it. Anyone seeing it knows exactly how I stand for Jesus. At times the pin has paved the way for me to share my testimony.

It is difficult, very difficult, to live a godly life beyond the confines of our own home. We have no choice but to cope with one another's dispositions and moods. There are bound to be conflicting opinions and capricious temperaments among the people with whom we work side by side. When someone behaves ambivalently toward me, I find it very disturbing, to say the least. It also bothers me a great deal when disagreements flare up and tempers are aroused, but all these things do happen, and there is very little I can do about it. Jesus said, "In the world ye shall have tribulation" (John 16:33), and these petty annoyances are all part of the world's tribulation. These are the "weeds of opposition" that sprout in the soil.

When confronted by anxiety-producing problems, I find I must withdraw momentarily into that quiet refuge deep within my innermost being where body, mind, and spirit meet, in order to regain spiritual strength and refreshment. I know that because of Christ's omnipotent presence, He is always with me, whether it be at work, at home, on a bus, or shopping.

He has every situation under control. He understands our problems, and He loves us, with all of our faults. He is our greatest and only Source of comfort, and He is the hope that is in us. Therein lies the answer to all our dilemmas.

In essence, one does not have to go off into secluded, cloistered exile and live in a continuous kneeling, prayerful posture in order to seek God and commune with Him. *He is wherever you are.* The most effectual prayers of petition, intercession, praise, and thanksgiving can go out at times when one is right in the midst of a trying situation.

Although my best prayer time is that quiet time when I am alone, most of my prayers are said during the day right in the middle of problems, for that is the time when I need the most help. Time spent waiting for a bus or standing on a long line can be used for meaningful prayer. Without a doubt, prayer has the power to renew, restore, and replenish the soul. Through prayer, one receives needed strength and encouragement to surmount all obstacles.

Fortunately for us, the good days far outnumber the bad and not-so-good ones. Remember, it takes the rain as well as the sun to make the flowers grow, so we too need some of the "rainy seasons." One of the first maxims we all learned in childhood was "April showers bring May flowers."

Have you ever inhaled the fragrance of a garden after the rain? The earth is cleansed, the sun shines, and all things appear fresh and new once more. Well, our "rainy seasons" afford an opportunity to make some new and important discoveries about ourselves and a chance to make a fresh start. We find out that we really are more hardy than we thought; we mature as a Christian and learn so much about God's grace, how sufficient it really is.

Today, thirty years after I accepted Christ, I am still an unfinished product. There is still a great deal to learn, a lot of room for improvement, and more weeding to be done. I am growing, mellowing, and learning how to place all my concerns in God's hands. I find myself speaking up more often and telling others what Jesus means to me. He *is* first in my life, and I enjoy sharing my faith.

> I am not ashamed of the gospel of Christ: for it is the power of God unto salvation to every one that believeth; to the Jew first, and also to the Greek.
>
> *Romans 1:16*

In order to be a faithful servant, the Christian's first duty is to confess Christ. In his letter to Timothy, Paul wrote,

> Be not thou therefore ashamed of the testimony of our Lord.
>
> *II Timothy 1:8*

The Psalmist wrote,

> Let the redeemed of the Lord say so.
>
> *Psalm 107:2*

And Jesus warned,

> No man, when he hath lighted a candle, putteth it in a secret place, neither under a bushel, but on a candle stick, that they which come in may see the light. . . . Take heed therefore that the light which is in thee be not darkness.
>
> *Luke 11:33, 35*

Beauty
from
ashes

Foothills and canyons in Southern California are dominated by dense vegetation consisting of several species of shrubby evergreens called *chaparral*. Some of the shrubs have roots extending underground to a depth of twenty feet seeking water because, unlike the cactus, this plant does not have the capacity to retain moisture.

Seeds from the chaparral flowers do not germinate when dropped, but they lie dormant in the soil for decades waiting for intense heat from a fire to break open the outer seed covering. It is amazing to learn that this shrub depends on fire to regenerate and ironically sets itself up to be the cause of that very fire.

One characteristic of this native vegetation is the high oil content in the leaves, which makes it extremely combustible. When preheated the plant emits gaseous vapors, making it potentially explosive.

While fire destroys most of the plant above ground, the tuberous roots below remain safe. In a matter of months after the fire, burls attached to the tubers begin sprouting and send up shoots, while the seeds dropped long ago begin to grow. Once again the chaparral thickets reappear with increased density to blanket the rugged terrain. In about fifteen years many of their branches begin to wither and die. These dry branches will become the dangerous fuel waiting to feed the next fire.

Early in November 1961, many factors conducive to creating a major inferno were present in Los Angeles. Due to a long period of severe drought, the moisture content of the vegetation covering the entire region was drastically reduced, making it highly susceptible to fire. Humidity was registered at a low of 4 percent, and hot, dry winds blowing in from the deserts caused unusually high temperatures, which hastened the drying of combustible materials. So threatening and hazardous were the conditions that residents used garden hoses and lawn sprinklers to water down the exteriors of their homes.

The fire department, aware of the mounting danger throughout the area, was already prepared. Every available man and every piece of equipment had been placed at strategic locations.

The worst fears were realized when an accidental fire erupted just below the summit of a brush-covered mountainous region. Hundreds of valuable homes nestled in the hillside lay in the path of the fire. Fanned by the santanas, or devil winds, and fueled by the dry brush, flames swept over the crest and down into Stone Canyon, engulfing the area in a raging inferno.

As firefighters battled the advancing wall of flames, high velocity winds carried burning debris beyond the perimeter of the main front, starting new fires at their backs. Danger from falling rocks, steep slopes, and interlocking thickets made firefighting even more hazardous. Flaming embers were showered into the air landing on buildings and igniting combustible roofing materials.

The ear-shattering roar and fury of the fire was unlike anything ever witnessed by the survivors. Although more than 400 homes were destroyed, no lives were lost, nor were there any serious injuries. This would go down in history as the most disastrous brush fire in Southern California.

Picture, if you will, several days later in the wake of the smoke and fire. Families return to the blackened remains of their homes. Their faces dazed with shock and disbelief. As they pick through the charred rubble in search of some cherished belonging, they can only find burned fragments of their once precious possessions. Some sit and stare at the blackened cinders, reliving those moments when they used garden hoses in a vain attempt to save their home until they were forced to flee, leaving everything but their lives to the voracious fire.

There is an epilogue to this story. Despite their loss and dispossession, these same families were able to rebuild new homes in exactly the same spot above the ashes and return again to the business of living. Why would anyone want to rebuild over ashes of their former home? Despite the risk of fire, these homeowners love the beautiful scenic area and have adapted to the unique climate of mild winters and long summers. This is where their roots are. This is where their friends and jobs are. This is home.

In this environment, human beings are the invaders and must respect the fact that unless they can think of ways to wipe out this dangerous vegetation, they must learn to live with it, just as many others have learned to live in volatile surroundings. Both can live together sharing the same plot of ground as long as man understands the problems and finds a workable solution.

Although the chaparral is burned out by fire, it too has its roots implanted in the soil. This is the land and climate to which it has adapted and to which it will return again and again. Without the chaparral, however, there would be considerable soil erosion, so it too does fill a need.

Proposals recommended by the fire department prior to the fire had to be considered. Ordinances were designed to reduce the existing hazardous conditions, because thousands of dwellings were being built in an area surrounded by potentially dangerous vegetation.

First of all, every small brush fire must be treated as a major fire before it has a chance to spread. Experience taught most homeowners to avoid using combustible roofing materials. There would have to be extensive brush clearance away from buildings, streets, and highways; use of less susceptible ground cover, wider fire breaks and wider streets with turning areas.

Ordinances were adopted regarding sprinkler systems and availability of more water for fire control. Once these measures were taken, people could live in their new homes, secure in the knowledge that every precaution was taken to prevent a recurrence of that fateful day in November 1961.

Bel Air and Brentwood are once again beautiful cities. Lush foliage and spacious lawns and gardens blanket the region with little evidence of the major conflagration two decades ago. This is beauty from ashes!

No matter what catastrophic circumstances people face, there is almost always a reconstructive aftermath. People are tougher than they give themselves credit for. Whether it be loss of home, loved ones, limbs, or even a job, each is a terrible disaster to the individual. But like the plants, there is a strong instinct to survive and restore life as quickly as possible. Without a doubt there is a period of despair and hopelessness when one cannot see beyond one's grief. But after the shock and the mourning, there is a desire to begin again and build beauty from ashes.

In another part of the world, in the jungles of South America, an Amazon Indian tribe discovered that beauty comes from ashes. They employ an agricultural method called "slash and burn." Before the rainy season begins, they select a site in the forest; cut down the underbrush to make a clearing; and then plant root crops consisting of sweet potatoes, taro, and manioc. When this planting has taken root, the men set fire to the piles of tinder-dry brush. The forest fire is maintained under watchful eye.

The whole purpose of this farming technique is to allow the plants to absorb essential nutrients from the ashes. About a week after the fire has burned out and cooled, they plant their remaining crops of papaya, bananas, cotton, and tobacco in the outer fringes where the soil contains a high nutrient count. Nutritious food rises from the ashes.

A city rises above the ashes, a forest rises above the ashes, and even people rise above the ashes. Survivors of tragedies often emerge from their ordeal with a brand-new outlook on life. During their long periods of recuperation, they have had time to reevaluate their goals and priorities. Some victims have heard the still small voice of God whispering encouragement. Some have been comforted by the Holy Spirit and discover that God has a better plan for their life. By their testimonies they offer inspiration and hope to fellow sufferers.

> Beloved, think it not strange concerning the fiery trial which is to try you, as though some strange thing happened unto you: But rejoice, inasmuch as ye are partakers of Christ's sufferings; that, when his glory shall be revealed, ye may be glad also with exceeding joy.
>
> *I Peter 4:12, 13*

So many of our contemporaries, courageous athletes, and young people have lost their limbs, yet they went on to become champions after their tragic accidents. They set goals and work hard at them until they are the best in the field. Read the inspiring stories of Joni Eareckson, who was left totally paralyzed after a diving accident, and Max Cleland, who lost his right arm and both legs in Vietnam. Discover how they became "more than conquerors" and "overcomers." Others like Diane Bringgold, Merrill Womack, and Norman Williams have literally been through the fire and survived.[25] They could have succumbed to a life of self-pity and hopeless despair, but instead they have all chosen to rise above the ashes and live victoriously. Through their ministries they now help many other people who have given up on life. They believed God's promises.

> When thou passeth through the waters, I will be with thee; and through the rivers, they shall not overflow thee; when thou walkest through the fire, thou shalt not be burned; neither shall the flame kindle upon thee.
>
> *Isaiah 43:2*

I am with thee: be not dismayed; for I am thy God; I will strengthen thee; yea, I will help thee.

Isaiah 41:10

Overcomers! That's just what the people of Peshtigo, Wisconsin, were in 1871. Stands of age-old conifers, such as white pine, spruce, cedar, balsam fir, and northern hardwood trees covered millions of acres. Here and there some scrubby jack pine, aspen, and scrub oak grew in the forest beside their more dominant neighbors. The lovely, deep forest was home for thousands of busy creatures. Birds chirped, deer roamed, squirrels foraged, beavers and chipmunks built their nests.

The lumber industry was thriving. Valuable trees large enough to supply wood for single homes were being felled. Sawmills and lumbermills buzzed as workers sliced trees into boards. Settlers lived in log cabins in clearings surrounded by small cultivated farms.

For several weeks the smell of smoke filled the crisp autumn air. Flakes of ashes fell like snow. The settlers knew that somewhere in the vast tinder-dry forest a ground fire was burning. Why did they not heed the warning—Where there's smoke there's fire? Surely the stinging of their eyes from the dense, smoky air should have been warning enough. But to the settlers, the fire seemed far away, out of reach. Due to a prolonged drought, the potential of a high-intensity fire existed.

Ground fires were smoldering for weeks, consuming the humus layer until eventually surface litter on the forest floor, undergrowth, and piles of dried slashings left by lumbermen caught fire. Foliage of tall trees dried out from the heat of the surface fires to a point where the leaves became highly combustible. The forest was now in danger of the worst fire of all—a crown fire. A spark from the burning embers was all that was needed to ignite the volatile leaves, causing them to explode and shower flaming brands in every direction. With the turbulence of a tornado, the fire raged beyond imagination, consuming everything in its path. Huge fireballs erupted into the sky, sending bits of burning debris in every direction. The holocaust continued until more than 2 million acres of beautiful virgin forest and more than 800 precious lives were lost. Who could foresee anything good resulting from this terrible disaster?

What never ceases to amaze or inspire me is the dauntless spirit with which survivors of catastrophies rebuild their lives so that the end result is better than it was in the first place. Within three years the face of the land in Peshtigo changed. Parts of the fire-cleared forest became farmland producing crops of wheat, oats, barley, and rye. The people took advantage of the leveled land and turned to farming and dairying. Instead of saw-mills, they built cheese factories.

Today the forest is once again famous for its wildlife. It is now a paradise for fishing and hunting. Peshtigo is still famous for its forest products. Besides paper products they manufacture commercial furniture, fixtures, and roofing beams. It is known as "the city that rose from the ashes."

Back in the burned-out forest many changes are taking place. The acres of devastated great white pine and hardwood trees are being replaced by scrubby jack pines. Fire is the only means of breaking open the seed pods of the jack pine cones, showering millions of seeds on the newly cleared forest floor. Instead of a few dozen jack pines among the acres of other trees that were standing before the fire, the forest now consists of millions of jack pine seedlings. They thrive because they are able to tolerate poor soil conditions and severe cold weather, nevertheless the jack pine ranks as an important timber and pulpwood tree.

Now that the fire has opened up large areas of ground to the light, other herbaceous plants will begin to sprout. From the cinders and ashes of the burned-out land a tall plant with deep magenta blossoms called *fireweed* appears. Whether the seeds have already been in the soil or whether they were carried by the wind and birds, they have finally found the ideal spot to begin growing. The nitrogen in the newly burned site stimulates the growth of the *fireweed*. In the first spring following a fire, annual herbs called *fire annuals* and *California poppies* blanket the hillsides. They will bloom for four or five more years and disappear when the shrubs have taken over. Their seeds will be carried in the wind or lie dormant until another fire sets them free. Many decades will pass before a second growth of the forest returns.

I want to conclude this chapter by asking, What will it take to burst the shell that has you bound? Will it take some heat to get you all fired up and set you free, or will it take some showers to make you grow and blossom like the flowers in the desert after the rain? Try to forget the past. Sure, it may have been rough. You may have been treated badly, and you may have had your problems, and perhaps you have every reason to be bitter—to withdraw into your shell—but the past is over. Let it go. What can you do now? Can you write, paint, teach, or sing? With God's help you can begin again. He will make a way where there was no way. Don't let others see only the despair and ashes, but let them see you as a beautiful being who rose victoriously above your circumstances.

Perhaps the best is yet to be. Before you think of giving up, ponder this little verse by Robert Browning.

> Grow old with me!
> The best is yet to be,
> The last of life,
> for which the first was made:
> Our times are in his hand
> Who saith, "A whole I planned,
> Youth shows but half;
> trust God: see all, nor be afraid.
>
> Robert Browning,
> "Rabbi Ben Ezra"[26]

Read the account of Job in the Old Testament. He lost everything—his home, children, servants, cattle, and friends. He was inflicted with great physical suffering and sat covered in ashes and sackcloth as was the custom of the time—ashes being a symbol of repentance—yet Job would never stop trusting God.

So the Lord blessed the latter end of Job more than his beginning.

Job 42:12

Beauty from ashes!

Greater love
hath no man

The showy trillium is a three-petaled white flower with three broad leaves surrounding the stem. This dainty flower arrives very early in spring and blooms in chilling winds, late snow, heavy rainfall, and sporadically hot days. Yet in spite of the inclement weather and harsh elements it faces, the trillium grows even more beautiful as it fades. Its pure white flowers turn to a fantastic shade of pink as it ages gloriously with grace, beauty, and character.

During our lifetime we all have had to face "harsh elements" at one time or another. Unforeseen problems suddenly appear, just like the strong winds and rain that beat upon the delicate flowers. After each downpour, new strength is added. We keep on growing through all kinds of "unsettling weather." Meanwhile characters are being molded, wisdom is being increased, and, most of all, we learn to keep on striving. We have weathered the storm, and we will survive the next.

> We are troubled on every side, yet not distressed; we are perplexed, but not in despair; Persecuted, but not forsaken; cast down, but not destroyed.
>
> *II Corinthians 4:8, 9*

One sunny afternoon in springtime, I made a special trip to the botanical garden in my neighborhood to take a snapshot of the pansies. When I arrived at the park, the gardener was watering that particular flower bed with a garden hose. When he finished, all the blossoms were soaked and drooping. Some were lying face down on the ground covered with wet dirt. They were totally devastated! There was nothing else I could do except stroll around the gardens and wait until the sun dried the flower bed.

When I returned much later, lo and behold, a most amazing and delightful sight greeted me! The pansies had perked up, literally bursting with renewed energy as they glistened in the sunshine. Not a vestige of their recent anguish was reflected on their faces. Cute little flowers they are! They actually wore smiles!

I was able to capture that precious event on the photo and now I keep the picture in a frame. It serves to remind me that the storms of life may threaten and weigh us down, and we may bend beneath the heavy burdens, but very soon the sunshine will reappear. Then we must rise to our feet, brush ourselves off, and greet the new day with expectation and hope.

With each crisis we experience, we become a little stronger, a little wiser, and a lot more patient. Hopefully, we have established a closer relationship with God through our pains and trials.

Look up at the sky when it's about to rain. The dark storm clouds are not standing still, they are moving very quickly, passing us by. Soon another day will dawn, flooding us with bright sunshine, perhaps even a rainbow in the clouds to confirm a new beginning.

A friend wrote this little verse when he was a small boy in the eighth grade. Even at this young and sensitive age he looked at the flower with keen insight, and it revealed to him the fact that endured suffering achieved patience:

I think that God's awesome power
Will do nothing better than a flower
A flower whose petals are colored
With the earth's changing seasons.
A flower that in summer heat

With bees buzzing honey sweet.
With stems dirt has lain
Which withstands every pain.
That's why I know
Flowers grow so slow.

Steven Marc Bernstein, "Flowers"[27]

Paul, in his letter to the Romans, put it this way:

> ... but we glory in tribulations also: knowing that tribulation work-
> eth patience; and patience, experience; and experience, hope:
> and hope maketh not ashamed; because the love of God is shed
> abroad in our hearts by the Holy Ghost which is given unto us.

Romans 5:3–5

Although we cannot understand why we hurt at times, perhaps there is a lesson to be learned from the tears and trials. This may be the time to get to know God better or to get to know ourselves better.

As parents, we must constantly discipline our children. We do not chastise our neighbor's children when they do wrong, but we only chide our own because we love them. We want to instruct them and correct them in order to develop their character. This is exactly the way God is dealing with us.

> For whom the Lord loveth he chasteneth, and scourgeth every
> son whom he receiveth. If ye endure chastening, God dealeth
> with you as with sons; for what son is he whom the father chas-
> teneth not?

Hebrews 12:6, 7

Look again at the first five words, "for whom the Lord loveth." My, the Lord must love you very much when He is taking the time to try you, to refine you, and reshape you. The potter breaks up the marred vessel, reshapes, remolds, and refires it until it is perfected and useful. God deals with you in the same manner. He cares about you, just as you care about your own loved ones.

The words from God that Moses delivered to the new generation of Israelites who grew up in the wilderness wanderings gave some insight concerning the reason for chastening:

> And thou shalt remember all the way which the Lord thy God led thee these forty years in the wilderness, to *humble* thee, and to *prove* thee, to know what was in thine heart, whether thou wouldest keep his commandments, or no.... Thou shalt also consider in thine heart, that as a man chasteneth his son, so the Lord thy God chasteneth thee.
>
> *Deuteronomy 8:2, 5*

In his second letter to the Corinthians, Paul reveals a very thought-provoking explanation of his own suffering. First of all, Paul had implored the Lord three times to remove the "thorn in his flesh," an imperfection in his life that surely must have weakened him physically. Any constant irritation, be it physical or mental, that pricks the pride or buffets the body is bound to take its toll on one's strength. It certainly caused Paul deep concern, or he would not have taken the trouble to make mention of it several times in his Epistles or to ask God three times to remove it. According to his own testimony, he spoke of these infirmities as being insults, hardships, persecutions, and distresses.

We all have faced one or more of these contentions during our lifetime, either separately or showered upon us all at one time, but how do we handle them? Do we glory in them? Are we happy when we are abused, insulted, ridiculed, intimidated, or in pain? Hardly. We become deeply distressed. However, Paul was able to say,

> I take pleasure in infirmities ... for when I am weak, then am I strong.
>
> *II Corinthians 12:10*

I could never quite grasp the meaning of this verse because it seemed almost contradictory to me. I would spend time pondering the words over and over. How could one be weak and yet strong? Recently, however, when I was wallowing in my own weakness during some very trying time, the interpretation became perfectly clear to me, and now I can apply the teaching to my own life.

Paul unfolds the text this way: "I have every reason to boast about myself and my accomplishments, for God has given me so much, and I would be a fool not to brag because it is the truth. However, in order to prevent me from becoming an arrogant and conceited fool, God inflicted me with a "thorn in the flesh," (a messenger from Satan) to wound my pride, and keep me from thinking more of myself than of Him." Here is the assurance from Christ Himself: "*My* power *works best* when *you* are *weak*." The more troubles I have, the more I need to depend upon the Lord; the more I am hurting, the more I have to go to Him to help me; and the more I go to Him, the more strength He pours on me. His power is made manifest in my weakness; thus, when I am weak I am stronger than ever *in Christ.*

And [the Lord] said to me, My grace is sufficient for thee; for my strength is made perfect in weakness. Most gladly therefore will I rather glory in my infirmities, that the power of Christ may rest upon me.... for when I am weak, then am I strong.

II Corinthians 12:9–10

Now that I have received greater understanding or call it, if you will, a spiritual revelation, of the meaning of the verse, I can have victory over anxiety. I call upon another power-packed Scripture to come to my aid when needed: "I can do everything [accomplish anything] through Him who gives me strength" (Philippians 4:13 NIV). Try it and know that it works.

Anytime God deals with us, it is for our enlightenment, to teach us, humble us, rid us of pride and vanity, test our faith, or bring us to our knees. He wants us to experience a closer walk with Him. We, with our finite minds, cannot begin to fathom what God, in His infinite wisdom, has in store for those who trust Him. Whatever your problem may be, you are bound to learn something from the experience. You may gain valuable insight and compassion from your distress that you never dreamed possible. You have acquired a firsthand knowledge and thus may be used of God as a channel to bring blessings into the life of another person going through the same kind of suffering. You will become a more effective servant after you have been tried and tested.

God heals hurts in many ways. One of the ways is to use people like you, who have been hurt, to work for Him by nurturing others.

> What a wonderful God we have—he is the Father of our Lord Jesus Christ, the source of every mercy, and the one who so wonderfully comforts and strengthens us in our hardships and trials. And why does he do this? So that when others are troubled, needing our sympathy and encouragement, we can pass on to them this same help and comfort God has given us.
>
> *II Corinthians 1:3, 4 LB*

Try to think back for a moment to a time when a friend confided in you the details of a terrible problem he or she was facing. Have you ever responded with the words, "The same thing happened to me, and it's really not as bad as you imagine"? By saying that, you are helping much more than you realize. So many organizations are springing up today in which groups of people sharing a common bond meet for therapy to assist one another until they can each stand alone. There are Alcoholics Anonymous, Parents without Partners, Parents of Missing Children, and many other groups of people helping people. By associating with the pain of another, one can truly comfort the grieving person.

Consider the Man Jesus when He was here on earth! There is not a single problem that you are facing that Jesus Himself did not personally suffer. He understands everything you are experiencing. Start with the lack of personal possessions: He had only the shoes on His feet and the clothes He wore. He had no home of His own during His ministry, only stones for a pillow. He had no means of transportation other than on foot, a few times by boat, and once on a donkey. The land He traveled had no paved roads or air-conditioned places to stop for a cool drink. He walked along the sun-baked, barren, and rocky wilderness and knew hunger and thirst. He was tempted, threatened, and acquainted with grief. His neighbors ridiculed Him so that He had to leave His home town. His best friends did not always understand Him. "What manner of Man is this?" they would say. One denied Him, and one betrayed Him. He was unjustly accused, slapped in the face, beaten, spit upon, scorned, mocked, tortured, and finally murdered. All of these tragic circumstances befell a Man who only cared about people's needs. He healed, fed, and loved *all* people. He even asked forgiveness for those who put Him to death. "Father, forgive them; for they know not what they do" (Luke 23:34).

Friend, you are never alone, God is a good God and a loving Father. If He can concern Himself with the lilies of the field, then He cares even more about you and your problems. Why, God loves you so much that

> he gave his only begotten son, that whosoever [meaning you] believeth in him should not perish, but have everlasting life.
>
> *John 3:16*

and Jesus, speaking of His love for us, said,

> Greater love hath no man than this, that a man lay down his life for his friends.
>
> *John 15:13*

He died that we might live, really live. What more can He do to prove how much He loves you and wants to help you, whatever your need may be?

What makest thou?

If you were to examine a handful of clay before a potter begins working on it, all you would see is a lumpy, ungainly mass of mud.

The skilled potter works on this pliable mass—shaping and forming it until the end result is a beautiful object, perhaps an urn, a pitcher, or a bowl. With each fresh batch of earth, the potter will fashion something different. Some of the objects will have spouts, some handles, some will hold water, and others will hold flowers. The potter makes bowls from which to eat, cook, wash, store supplies, and burn oil. Each is destined to serve some special purpose.

The potter kneads the wet clay for several hours to remove all the air bubbles and then sets it on a spinning disk. By hand the potter gently hollows out the mass of clay while it spins. With gentle touches of his fingers, the vessel begins to take the desired shape inside and out.

Some finishing touches are in order before it is fired. The potter may want to fill some pores, buff it to a shine, or paint decorations on it. Finally, the clay object is ready to be fired in high temperatures that will change the physical and chemical properties into a new stonelike substance.

Each vessel the potter creates receives special, individualized care. Although each one varies in shape, size, and color, all have been kneaded, shaped, and decorated by the master's skilled hands and finally fired in the oven. The end result is a beautiful, useful vessel.

I used to tell the following story to the children in my Sunday school class:

> There was a handful of clay in the bank of a river. It was only common clay, coarse and heavy; but it had high thoughts of its own value, and wonderful dreams of the great place which it was to fill in the world when the time came for its virtues to be discovered.
>
> Overhead, in the spring sunshine, the trees whispered together of the glory which descended upon them when the delicate blossoms and leaves began to expand, and the forest glowed with fair, clear colours, as if the dust of thousands of rubies and emeralds were hanging, in soft clouds, above the earth.
>
> The flowers, surprised with the joy of beauty, bent their heads to one another, as the wind caressed them, and said: "Sisters, how lovely you have become. You make the day bright."
>
> The river, glad of new strength and rejoicing in the unison of all its waters, murmured to the shores in music, telling of its release from icy fetters, its swift flight from the snow-clad mountains, and the mighty work to which it was hurrying—the wheels of many mills to be turned, and great ships to be floated to the sea.
>
> Waiting blindly in its bed, the clay comforted itself with lofty hopes. "My time will come," it said. "I was not made to be hidden forever. Glory and beauty and honor are coming to me in due season."
>
> One day the clay felt itself taken from the place where it had waited so long. A flat blade of iron passed beneath it, and lifted it, and tossed it into a cart with other lumps of clay, and it was carried far away, as it seemed, over a rough and stony road. But it was not afraid, nor discouraged, for it said to itself: "This is

necessary. The path to glory is always rugged. Now I am on my way to play a great part in the world."

But the hard journey was nothing compared with the tribulation and distress that came after it. The clay was put into a trough and mixed and beaten and stirred and trampled. It seemed almost unbearable. But there was consolation in the thought that something very fine and noble was certainly coming out of all this trouble. The clay felt sure that, if it could only wait long enough, a wonderful reward was in store for it.

Then it was put upon a swiftly turning wheel, and whirled around until it seemed as if it must fly into a thousand pieces. A strange power pressed it and moulded it, as it revolved, and through all the dizziness and pain it felt that it was taking a new form.

Then an unknown hand put it into an oven, and fires were kindled about it—fierce and penetrating—hotter than all the heats of summer that had ever brooded upon the bank of the river. But through all, the clay held itself together and endured its trials, in the confidence of a great future. "Surely," it thought, "I am intended for something very splendid, since such pains are taken with me. Perhaps I am fashioned for the ornament of a temple, or a precious vase for the table of a king."

At last the baking was finished. The clay was taken from the furnace and set down upon a board, in the cool air, under the blue sky. The tribulation was passed. The reward was at hand.

Close beside the board there was a pool of water, not very deep, not very clear, but calm enough to reflect, with impartial truth, every image that fell upon it. There for the first time, as it was lifted from the board, the clay saw its new shape, the reward of all its patience and pain, the consummation of its hopes—a common flower pot, straight and stiff, red and ugly. And then it felt that it was not destined for a king's house, nor for a palace of art, because it was made without glory or beauty or honour; and it murmured against the unknown maker, saying, "Why hast thou made me thus?"

Many days it passed in sullen discontent. Then it was filled with earth, and something—it knew not what—but something rough and brown and dead-looking, was thrust into the middle of the earth and covered over. The clay rebelled at this new disgrace. "This is the worst of all that has happened to me, to be filled with dirt and rubbish. Surely I am a failure."

But presently it was set in a greenhouse, where the sunlight fell warm upon it, and water was sprinkled over it, and day by day as it waited, a change began to come to it. Something was stirring within it—a new hope. Still it was ignorant, and knew not what the new hope meant.

One day the clay was lifted again from its place, and carried into a great church. Its dream was coming true after all. It had a fine part to play in the world. Glorious music flowed over it. It was surrounded with flowers. Still it could not understand. So it whispered to another vessel of clay, like itself, close beside it, "Why have they set me here? Why do all the people look toward us?" And the other vessel answered, "Do you not know? You are carrying a royal sceptre of lilies. Their petals are white as snow, and the heart of them is like pure gold. The people look this way because the flower is the most wonderful in the world. And the root of it is in your heart."

Then the clay was content, and silently thanked its maker, because, though an earthen vessel, it held so great a treasure.

Henry van Dyke, "A Handful of Clay"[28]

God made each of us in the same painstaking way, giving special care and attention to creating a lovely, useful vessel.

Let me tell you something about one vessel that the Lord made—myself. I was introduced to Jesus at the age of four by my earthly father, who taught me my first bedtime prayer. He told me how Jesus loved me and watched over me day and night. Although I was very young, I became conscious of Jesus from that time on and believed with all my mind that He was always watching me.

Along with my brother and sister, I was enrolled in the primary department of the local church, and from then on, my entire childhood was dominated by churchgoing. I loved Sunday school because all of my friends were there. We all grew up together in the church, going to all the Sunday school grades, Wednesday prayer meetings, Thursday choir practices, and Sunday night Christian Endeavor. The church sponsored two-week summer vacations for us at Christian Herald and Volunteers of America camps for boys and girls.

Thanks to loving, dedicated teachers I received an excellent head knowledge of the Bible, but I still had not grasped the fundamental truth that I had to accept Christ into my heart as well in order to receive eternal life.

My moment of new birth came at the age of nineteen while listening to Charles Fuller's "Old Fashioned Revival Hour" on the radio, aired from the Municipal Auditorium in Long Beach, California. The message of salvation was made clear to me and at the invitation, I accepted Christ. This moment was unlike anything I had ever experienced. I now knew Christ in a different way than I had known Him in the past. This was a personal, heart knowledge.

Almost everyone believes that there was a Person called Jesus. I always knew He was there, somewhere. But to accept Him into our heart is quite different from just knowing *about* Him. In a previous chapter I mentioned that Paul, before his conversion, could not accept the belief that one Man's death on the cross could take away the sins of many, and he persecuted those who did believe this. Later, when he too became a believer, God used him in a most remarkable way.

Let me tell you about the conversion Paul experienced and how simple it is for anyone to receive Christ. First of all, Jesus said,

Except a man be born again, he cannot see the kingdom of God.

John 3:3

Born again? Yes, but this is a spiritual rebirth. What does one have to do? One only has to believe that Jesus died in propitiation for our sins.

In the Old Testament, a spotless male lamb without blemish (Leviticus 1:10) had to be sacrificed as a blood offering to atone for the sins of the individual. In the New Testament, Jesus was the perfect, spotless, innocent Lamb of God, sacrificed as a final blood offering to redeem the sins of the world (Hebrews 9:13–28).

Here is a very simple illustration: When my brother and I were very small, we played with a large magnet, picking up nails, paper clips, and pins. One day we found some metal dust resembling particles of sand. We waved the magnet over the metal fragments and they would instantly swoop up and cling tight to the magnet. In the same way, when Jesus was nailed to the cross, all of our sins were swept up with Him. There at the cross His atoning blood cleansed those sins away forever—"He bare the sin of many" (Isaiah 53:12). Jesus did all of this for us so that we could inherit the free gift of eternal life.

> God ... gave his only begotten Son, that whosoever believeth in him should not perish, but have everlasting life.
>
> *John 3:16*

One cannot buy salvation at any price. This is freely given and freely received. The New Testament is Jesus' last will and testament. When he died, He left us an inheritance. All one has to do to claim it is to believe in Christ's atoning blood, then as heirs, we become joint heirs to the Kingdom and God's *free* gift of salvation.

> ... now being made free from sin, and become servants to God, ye have your fruit unto holiness, and the end everlasting life. For the wages of sin is death; but the gift of God is eternal life through Jesus Christ our Lord.
>
> *Romans 6:22, 23*

Before conversion we just know *about* Him, but afterward we *know* Him. To know Jesus is to *love* Him and to *know* He loves us. This love is bigger, it is better, and it is forever. This love brings no broken hearts and no broken promises. This love is a miracle, and a miracle is something God does for you. But you have a part to play in it too. First of all, you must want it. Then you have to tell Him you regret all the wrong you have done and you want Him to come into your life. Then the miracle happens! The Holy Spirit fills your being, and you are reborn, made new, washed in the blood. You are now heir to eternal life. This is an experience you never had before and you will never have again.

People give testimonies of miraculous changes in their lives or miraculous healings. Some will believe the truth with all their heart, while skeptics will frown with tongue in cheek. Unless you have actually been born again, you cannot comprehend the depth of this personal experience. You only have to take God's Word for it that after you receive this new life in Christ something good will happen to you.

At the moment I accepted Christ, I did not receive the gift of tongues nor was I baptized in the Spirit as others are. Nor were there any dramatics or hysterics, but a quiet, reverent union with God as though a light went on and the darkness was gone. I was filled with a deep abiding love of Jesus that stayed with me and held onto me all through the years. This love has grown deeper and better through the years.

During our teen years, my friends and I attended Jack Wyrtzen's rallies every Saturday night in Manhattan. Jack's "Word of Life" radio program originated from the Gospel Tabernacle on Eighth Avenue. After the rallies, we held our own little street meetings in Times Square, giving out tracts, singing hymns, and giving our testimonies. We offered to pray with any passerby who requested prayer, and we answered their questions about the Bible as well as we knew how. There were also a lot of jeers to contend with. One friend had a good answer when some heckler shouted, "Go on, you're cracked in the head!" "Sure," he answered, "but that's when the Light came in." Several of us took night courses at a theological seminary for two years and attended seminars and conferences.

We spent summer vacations at Camp-of-the-Woods and Word of Life Island. Both are Christian family camps in the

Adirondack Mountains. Our church leaders were dedicated people whose efforts were directed toward leading the young people in the right direction.

Late on Sunday nights, after coming home from Christian Endeavor meetings, my sister and I would listen to several of the evangelistic radio programs before retiring. One of the young evangelists was a minister named Oral Roberts; another was Ralph Montanus of the Gospel Association for the Blind, whose program is called "That They Might See," and still another was Billy Graham, whose program is called "Hour of Decision." That was back in the late 1940s. Praise God, these men are still devotedly serving the Lord today and continue to win millions to Christ all over the world.

Eventually my friends at church accepted Christ one by one. We taught Sunday school, sang in the choir, worked on the church newspaper, and engaged in other church activities. Most of us married within our own congregation and soon all went our separate ways. That was more than thirty years ago.

All the ingredients for a useful vessel were there to start with, but what a waste, for this vessel did not serve its purpose!

Woe unto him that striveth with his Maker! . . . Shall the clay say to him that fashioneth it, What makest thou?

Isaiah 45:9

And the vessel was marred in the hands of the potter

I still kept the faith, but unfortunately I kept it a secret. Faith needs to be put into operation, for without works it is dead. Some remodeling of this vessel was definitely in order. It appears that the Word that came to the prophet Jeremiah may even relate to me.

> Then I went down to the potter's house, and, behold, he wrought a work on the wheels. And the vessel that he made of clay was marred in the hand of the potter: so he made it again another vessel, as seemed good to the potter to make it.... Behold, as the clay is in the potter's hand, so are ye in mine hand.
>
> *Jeremiah 18:3, 4, 6*

Thirty years had gone by since Christ came into my heart, and I realized that I had done very little for Him in all those years. It was about time for me to begin to be of service to Him.

My life was beginning to undergo a series of physical and emotional alterations. God, in His goodness, released the ties that had me bound so long, and I was set free.

Liberated woman? Yes, in a sense I became a liberated

woman. I have been freed from the fears that inhibited me, freed from anxiety, loneliness, self-pity, and self-imposed limitations.

The Lord replaced these with new concepts of positive-thinking. I have peace of mind, self-confidence, and faith that God will always take care of my needs.

The first cataclysmic change was that now we had become a single-parent family, and there is no need to say how difficult it was to live on a fraction of our accustomed income. Fortunately, I had recently returned to work and, small as it was, at least there was a salary coming in every week.

My boys were in high school. The oldest was a senior, and his needs at the time were greater than in all of the previous school years. There were added expenses of senior prom, senior ring, graduation, driver training, and, of course, more food and clothes than ever before.

We found ourselves learning to pray together, and the phrase "let's pray about it" became part of our daily rhetoric. For where else was there to turn for help, but to the Lord? Somehow, God met all of our needs through this difficult time, and we never lacked the essentials.

> Behold the fowls of the air: for they sow not, neither do they reap, nor gather into barns; yet your heavenly Father feedeth them. Are ye not much better than they?
>
> *Matthew 6:26*

My oldest son went into the service right after graduation, and our family circle was down to two. We reached out to God as never before, and He became the Head of our home. No decision was made without asking Him first. When problems came, we left nothing to chance, but drew closer to God and to each other. This was the greatest period of spiritual growth that our family ever experienced. We were upheld by the Holy Spirit during this time of separation, and prayers were answered in the most timely and specific manner.

While at boot camp my son wrote that his faith in the Lord was the only thing that sustained him. The physical training and hours of marching in the hot July and August temperatures in Florida were enough to try anyone's faith, but he got through it and is the better for it.

As if things weren't bad enough, I lost my job and was now among the unemployed. I want to add here that losing a job unexpectedly is a very devastating experience, but even though it was a financial setback and a time of crisis, I remember thinking that it was one less decision I had to make. I did not like the job I had and was reluctant to leave. Losing a job can be a means of releasing you for something much better. In my case it was.

The next ten weeks were spent in fruitless search for work. Secretarial jobs were plentiful in New York City, but I did not want to work so far from my home in the suburbs. I was trying to find a job close by. However, clerical positions in my local area were scarce. Those that were available offered low pay and no fringe benefits, which were important to me now as the head of the household.

Working in the city meant a long bus ride to the subway and then another forty minutes on the subway. If connections were not good, it would take close to three hours a day traveling, and I did not want to spend so much time commuting back and forth every day. What a dilemma this was! The outlook remained dim and uncertain, and my prayers took on a new dimension.

I felt a great longing to be with people who could give me a spiritual boost; at the same time I felt burdened to do something useful for Christ.

Since there were some days when I had no appointments for job interviews and lots of spare time on my hands, I called a Christian organization for the blind to see if they could use some voluntary help. In answer to prayer, the librarian did need help. For a very short time, only a few hours a day, a few days a week, I worked in their office, typing and doing small clerical chores in the Braille library. What a tremendous blessing and spiritual lift I received, much more than I gave. At a time when I was really dejected, the librarian became my new friend who reached out with compassion and prayed for me. Sometimes a person comes into your life at precisely the right moment, speaking words that you really need to hear. You never know how much your help can mean to someone when they are feeling depressed.

Two months had gone by, and I desperately needed to find work soon. I was listening to Reverend Oral Roberts on television as I had been doing every week for many years. This particular morning, however, his message seemed to be directed right at me, because what he was saying was almost as though he knew about my problem. He prayed for someone who was out of work and said, "Something good is going to happen to you. Your miracle is about to begin, and it will begin today."[29] What happened next was nothing short of a series of miracles.

On the couch next to me was the *New York Times*. The Sunday edition has a separate section for job advertisements, and this section was folded open beside me. As I looked down, I saw exactly the kind of work that suited me, and, even though it was in the City, it interested me, so I tore off the corner of the page. The next morning I went into the City and applied for the job, but to my disappointment the position was not what I expected. The interviewer was ready to hire me immediately, but I told her that I must think about it and would call back in one hour. I walked along Fifth Avenue and went into the public library to sit for a few minutes while deciding what to do next. In my pocket was the small section of want ads that I had ripped from the paper. As I looked for the phone number to call the office I just left, I noticed that a few words still remained for the next ad, but most of it had been torn away. "Religious Organization, Typist . . ." and a phone number were all that remained. I know that the Holy Spirit led me to that position. It was more than I hoped for, a religious organization devoted to helping people and serving God.

The experience taught me that when we impose limits on ourselves, God cannot use us effectively. He will never force us to go where we do not want to go, but if we leave it up to Him, there is no limit to what He will help us to accomplish for ourselves.

The months that followed turned out to be a growing spiritual experience for me. I now had an opportunity to begin again, set some short-term goals, establish lasting friendships and a whole new set of values with eternity in view. There was one lady whose special friendship I will always cherish. We soon became good friends and prayer partners. She invited me to a Full Gospel Businessmen's Fellowship luncheon with her one Saturday at the Statler Hotel in New York City. What a pleasure it was to be in that company, surrounded by praying, believing Christians who sang hymns, gave marvelous testimonies of changed lives and healings, and rejoiced in praising the Lord. There was no doubt that God was opening the windows of heaven and showering me with blessings.

Six months after I started working there, I suddenly became ill and was taken to a hospital for an operation. This may not seem like much of a miracle, but to me it was just that! Had this happened only a few months earlier, it would have proven to be a financial and mental disaster. God's timing is never too early and never too late. First, He found this job for me, and just in the nick of time I was covered by all the medical benefits. While in the hospital, my faith was being put to the test, and I was given the most wonderful opportunity to witness for the Lord. This was indeed a brand-new venture in possibility thinking. God does things in such a wonderful way.

In the weeks I spent recuperating, I never had to worry about the financial aspects of the hospitalization, so my mind was at peace. There was something else I had gained and that was all the new friends that came into my life—wonderful, caring people who helped to make my life so rich. Never before did I receive so many letters, phone calls, flowers, and visits. Blessings were being poured on me daily, and the renewing and transforming continued. The weeks I spent at home gave me ample time to develop a deeper relationship with Christ through prayer, meditation, and Bible reading. My new friend from the library sent me a card with these words that expressed my feelings exactly:

I needed the quiet so He drew me aside.
Into the shadows where we could confide.

Away from the bustle where all the day long
I hurried and worried when active and strong.

I needed the quiet tho at first I rebelled
But gently, so gently, my cross He upheld
And whispered so sweetly of spiritual things
Tho weakened in body, my spirit took wings
To heights never dreamed of when active and gay.
He loved me so greatly He drew me away.

I needed the quiet. No prison my bed,
But a beautiful valley of blessings instead—
A place to grow richer in Jesus to hide.
I needed the quiet so He drew me aside.

Alice Hansche Mortenson, "I Needed the Quiet"[30]

Thanks be to God I am not the same after these experiences nor will I ever be. He had done so much for me, even though I did so very little for Him for so long. Apart from God I cannot exist.

I am crucified with Christ: nevertheless I live; yet not I, but Christ liveth in me.

Galatians 2:20

Now, I can no more walk away from Him than I can walk away from my shadow on a sunny day.

And he made it again another vessel, as seemed good to the potter to make it.

Jeremiah 18:4

All that I have is yours

God placed all the lovely flowering plants and trees here on earth to beautify, to enrich, to heal, and to nourish, but He gave us much, much more. We read in Scripture, "Ask, and it shall be given you" (Matthew 7:7).

This, of course, does not mean that we are to ask and then sit back and wait for everything to be handed to us. We must work, plant seeds of faith, search the Scriptures, trust, listen, and obey. By His grace, we are each given certain attributes—a mind to think, the physical capability to work, our own two hands, and the know-how to tackle a job. It is up to us to utilize these gifts He has given us and to set goals for ourselves.

Self-support, self-fulfillment, and dependent children are strong motivators. Above all, a desire to be obedient to God and to please Him helps us to be the best we can be. In his second letter to the Thessalonians, Paul wrote,

> If a man will not work, he shall not eat. We hear that some among you are idle. . . . Such people we command and urge in the Lord Jesus Christ, to settle down and earn the bread they eat.
>
> *II Thessalonians 3:10–12 NIV*

God provides the channels by opening doors to job opportunities so that we can work to earn the money to get the things we need. How we spend our money and what we buy is our decision.

> Every man should eat and drink, and enjoy the good of all his labor, it is the gift of God.
>
> *Ecclesiastes 3:13*

There is no limit to the abundance that God has for those who love and trust Him. His supply is without limit. It is there for the asking. He owns the cattle on a thousand hills and as joint heirs with Christ, they are ours too, if we believe in Him.

When God said to Solomon, "Ask what I shall give thee," Solomon asked only for wisdom.

> Give therefore thy servant an understanding heart to judge thy people, that I may discern between good and bad: for who is able to judge this thy so great a people? And the speech pleased the Lord, that Solomon had asked this thing. And God said,... Because thou hast asked this thing, and hast not asked for thyself long life, neither hast asked riches for thyself ... I have given thee a wise and understanding heart.... And I have also given thee that which thou hast not asked, both riches, and honor; so that there shall not be any among the kings like unto thee all thy days.
>
> *I Kings 3:9–13*

King Solomon desperately needed God's help in using good judgment. He felt that by himself he was not equal to the seemingly overwhelming task that lay before him. Above all, Solomon eagerly sought God's help to be a wise, discerning ruler over the chosen people. God granted his request, giving him the wisdom he sought, but also added material wealth beyond imagination.

> But thou shalt remember the Lord thy God; for it is he that giveth thee power to get wealth.
>
> *Deuteronomy 8:18*

Many a millionaire started with little money, but had an idea, a dream, and the faith to take a giant step with the little he had and spiral it into a fortune. The late Colonel Harland Sanders of Kentucky-Fried-Chicken fame had little more than a dream to begin with and a mountain-moving faith. His name is now a household word to millions of people.

William Newton Clark said, "Faith is the daring of the soul to go further than it can see,"[31] and Paul declared, "We walk by faith not by sight" (II Corinthians 5:7).

In the Old Testament, Abraham walked by faith and not by sight from Ur of the Chaldees to the land of Canaan. God told him to take his family and belongings and move to a new, unknown land that would be an inheritance to him and all his descendants. Abraham was obedient to God, following Him across deserts and plains, until he reached the Promised Land. Along the way, his flocks and herds multiplied, and he became not only a wealthy and respected man, but the father of many nations.

Moses obeyed God and led the Israelites through the wilderness for forty years by faith alone. Noah obeyed God's instructions without question and spent 120 years building the ark, which was half the size of the *Queen Mary*. He never gave up although he was laughed at, ridiculed, and never won a single convert to the Lord. Only when he and his family and the animals were safely inside the ark with the door shut tight and the rains descended, did the people outside finally believe what Noah had been preaching for so long, but it was too late. They assumed the attitude of "seeing is believing" or "show me and then I will believe." True faith reverses the cliché to "believing is seeing."

> Hope that is seen is no hope at all. Who hopes for what he already has? But if we hope for what we do not yet have, we wait for it patiently.
>
> *Romans 8:24, 25 NIV*

> Faith is the substance of things hoped for, the evidence of things not seen.
>
> *Hebrews 11:1*

133

Do you have an idea rolling about in your head, to start a new business, to make a change in your career, or to begin again at something new, somewhere else? Just as the snowball rolled in the snow begins to grow as big as you want to make it, so your idea will begin to snowball with God's help. Believe in your idea first. Visualize it coming to pass. Talk it over with Him, then be still and listen to His directions. I have heard this referred to as "listening with the ear of faith." Answers will come in unexpected ways, and you must be ready and willing to accept them. Then put your thoughts into action, for faith without works is dead.

The very fact that you are now reading this book is proof that faith and prayer work miracles. I believed in an idea, visualized it, talked it over with God, and followed the plan by doing something about it. God gave my prayer substance by making my dream a reality.

One of the ways God answers prayers is by planting new thoughts and ideas into your mind. It is important to be receptive and to respond to these ideas in a positive manner. It may well be that the Holy Spirit is at work changing your thinking. If you keep your mind open, constructive thoughts will rise, a new spirit of enthusiasm will flow in and release some of the negativity that has been holding you back.

These can be life-changing thoughts. Your new optimistic outlook will spark a new vitality and energy, thus turning your life around for the better.

When we offer a prayer to the Lord, it is very much like planting seeds. Saint Francis of Assisi wrote: "Don't look backward. A farmer doesn't look back when he sows. Sow! and just let God provide the rain and good weather."[32] When we plant a seed in a flower pot, there are no visible signs for a very long time, but we know without a doubt that there is action going on behind the scenes. We keep it in the sun and water it daily. Underneath the soil the seed is absorbing the moisture and beginning to swell. We do not dig it up periodically to check its growth. We just have to believe and trust that a miracle is taking place.

Soon the seed cracks open, and the root starts its descent downward, as it struggles beneath the soil and out of sight. It may take days, weeks, or months before the green sprout appears. There is nothing we can do but keep on watering and waiting patiently. Meanwhile the root is growing, feeding, and nourishing the plant through the stem, preparing it for that bright, sunny day when it will reveal to the world its lovely, fragrant flower.

This is the way we must believe that our prayers are being answered. We have told the Lord our needs and desires, now we must wait for the answer. We may never know how God is working behind the scenes, preparing a person or persons, making a new way where there was no way before. Doors are being opened to let in the good, and doors are being closed to shut out the bad. While all this activity is taking place, unknown to us, we must rest in the Lord, believe, and wait expectantly. All we can do is trust the Father that an answer is on the way.

> Without faith it is impossible to please Him; for he that cometh to God must believe that He is, and that He is a rewarder of them that diligently seek Him.
>
> *Hebrews 11:6*

Do you sometimes wonder why your prayers seem to go no further than your walls or ceiling? Do you feel that your prayers go unanswered in spite of your pleas, and do you think perhaps you are not getting through to God? If anxious thoughts are bombarding your mind at a feverish pace; if worry, conflict, and frustration are at a boiling point, then how can you expect to hear when God answers you? His voice cannot be heard above the din of your troubled mind. You can be sure that He is there when you call. "He is not far from each one of us" (Acts 17:27 NIV). He is trying to reach you and to calm you, but you have built a dense wall of noise and chaos through which the peace of God cannot penetrate. This age-old, well-worn precept has been tried and tested and proven to work: "Let go and let God." Once you let go of your burdens and your thoughts settle down, you will experience a sense of peace enfolding you. Quietness will flow in where pressure prevailed. In this peaceful, unhurried frame of mind, a channel will open up through which you can now communicate with God and He with you. Allow Him to guide your thinking.

The solution to your problems may not appear like a bolt of lightning out of the blue, although it's not impossible. What is more likely to happen is that in the light of this inner peace you will see your problems from a different perspective. You once had an all-consuming fear that the situation was about to destroy you. Now God is in control of the matter.

God has endowed man with the ability to use plain common sense in decision making, but when the mind is beset with struggles, the intellect is pushed into the background and confusion takes over.

Once attuned to God, you have consciously established unhurried, clearer thinking, and you are able to see your problems from another vantage point. Thus, by keeping the channels flowing, He can help you to work out the solution by yourself. This too is an answer.

Sometimes the scenes in our mind bear a striking resemblance to a battle zone, with anxious thoughts exploding to the left and right. Replays of a thousand events are crossfiring, and a rapid succession of questions are bombarding us from every side: "Why didn't I?" "What's the use?" "What can I do?" "Where can I turn?" "Why?" "How?" "What if . . . ?" "Will relief ever come?"

God seems so far above this dreadful strife, and we seem to be cowering beneath the roar, unable to see Him through the thick veil of darkness. I am writing from my own experience. I know what you are feeling, and it is frightening. For the sake of saying something comforting, I won't offer the redundant clichés that one hears so often, such as, "Don't worry, it will all work out." What I want to convey to fellow sufferers is a message from the Father to assure you that help is on the way, if you seek it and believe it to be so.

Remember how the disciples were out in a boat one night and a sudden storm caused raging winds and waves that filled the boat with water, tossing it about in the sea? Who wouldn't be scared under those conditions? They cried out, "Lord, save us, we perish," and Jesus, who was sleeping in the boat, woke up and said, "Why are ye fearful, O ye of little faith?" He immediately proceeded to rebuke the wind and the sea, and there was a great calm (see Matthew 8:23–26). He did not take them out of the water, but He calmed the water around them.

A similar scene took place later on in Matthew, Chapter 14. Jesus told the disciples to get into a ship and to go to the other side while He sent the multitudes away. He then went up into a mountain alone to pray.

During the night, in the middle of the sea, the wind and waves tossed the ship about, and the men aboard feared for their lives. At that moment, Jesus was walking on the sea toward them. Thinking Him to be some sort of spirit, the disciples were alarmed. He called out reassuringly, "Be of good cheer, it is I, be not afraid" (Matthew 14:27). Peter, needing more assurance, answered, "If it is you, let me walk on the water to meet you." Fortified by an initial flux of faith, Peter got out of the ship to go to Jesus, but as soon as he saw with his "visual sight" that he was actually standing alone in the turbulence, he panicked and began to sink, shouting, "Lord, save me." Jesus must have been very close by this time, because He reached out His hand and caught Peter and uttered almost the same words He said during the previous sea venture, "O thou of little faith, wherefore didst thou doubt?" In spite of Peter's meager amount of faith on this occasion, Jesus helped him into the ship and calmed the sea once more.

Bear in mind that our help comes from the same Lord the disciples called on. He is the same today as He was then, and He will be tomorrow. If He heard their frantic cries through the stormy, crashing sea and brought them peace, then He can hear your frantic cries through the raging billows that toss you about. He will reach out His hand toward you and calm the tempest that engulfs you.

Do you think it takes some kind of superhuman faith to believe that He can perform wonders in your life? No, it does not! Twice Jesus said to the frightened disciples, "Ye of *little* faith," and then He granted their requests, and gave them the peace they sought. If you have *any* faith at all, then you must use it, and each time you do, you will find it growing in proportion to your need.

A person who has never practiced cannot run a marathon. It takes years of training, as does any sport. The muscles have to be gradually exercised day after day before one can run a race or compete in sports. Faith too, has to be used constantly and put to practice day after day in all circumstances, great and small. Not even the Bible heroes of the past started out with enormous portions of faith. They were all ordinary people, and all had some measure of faith to begin with. But depending on how much they used it and how much they trusted God, their faith sustained them and helped them to accomplish great things.

> Who through faith subdued kingdoms, wrought righteousness, obtained promises, stopped the mouths of lions. Quenched the violence of fire, escaped the edge of the sword, out of weakness were made strong, waxed valiant in fight, turned to flight the armies of the aliens.
>
> *Hebrews 11:33, 34*

There is a power in faith that can accomplish the impossible. As I say this to you, I am endeavoring to reinforce my own faith. In other words, I always have to "practice what I preach," because I too need this kind of help every day of my life for all my mistakes and shortcomings.

Perhaps you may think, "What does she know of the pressures brought to bear by great financial stress?" But I do know. I have been there. Years ago my husband and I had to move from our home with a mountain of debts. We were young and deeply in debt to loan companies, banks, and department stores. We owed money to family and friends and never thought we could ever repay our debts. At the time, my husband was unemployed and recuperating from surgery. Our youngest child had recently recovered from surgery, and our other child spent one month in another hospital. Since we had no hospital insurance coverage at the time, we were even indebted to hospitals and doctors. For a long time there seemed to be no way out of the dilemma and the despair brought on by sickness, worry, and dispossession. Those were desperate days when all seemed bleak and hopeless. My husband eventually got well, started a new job, and every week a large portion of his salary was set aside toward paying the old debts while we lived frugally on the balance. In a few years, all of the debts were paid in full.

The most difficult part was not repaying the money, but the decision as to how to begin again, find a job, and establish a new way of living and spending. It can be done.

You may think, "What does she know about the pain of having a loved one who is an alcoholic?" But I do know, I have been there.

You may think, "What does she know about the devastation of divorce?" But I do know, I have been there too, after a twenty-five-year marriage. None of these problems are too hard for God. He *will* solve them, even if it means giving you the knowledge and the wherewithal to work them out for yourself.

For me, the answers do not come easily. I hear no loud, clear voice telling me what I should do. Usually, I have to read the Bible, pray, read again, and pray some more for several days. I must spend as many hours as I can in silence, reading His Word and paying undivided attention to what the Word is saying. Lo and behold, a time comes when one verse seems to stand out from all the rest, and on that I base the answer. Many times, I am left on my own with no recognizable answer, and logic has to take over.

I believe prayer is more instant than a telegraph signal, for when you pray, things begin to happen and answers are already on the way, although you are not aware of them at the moment.

Before they call, I will answer; and while they are yet speaking, I will hear.

Isaiah 65:24

139

By the grace of God, the power of prayer, and the intervention of the Holy Spirit, two near tragedies involving both of my sons were averted.

When my older boy was stationed at a naval base in Virginia, he called to tell me that he would be coming home for the weekend. His friend had a car, and they planned on driving home. As always, I turned to God and asked Him to send His guardian angels to keep them safe every mile of the way home. I know most mothers are concerned when their children are out in a car. For some reason, just before getting ready for the journey, my son was assigned to weekend duty aboard ship, and at the last minute his leave was canceled.

The young man with the car started out on his own, and on the way he picked up a hitchhiker. Unfortunately, they had a terrible accident in which the hitchhiker was killed instantly and the driver so seriously injured that months later he was medically discharged from the service. Though I deeply regret that the accident occurred at all, the impact of that answer to prayer will never be forgotten.

The following summer, my younger son, David, who had never been away from home on a long trip, made plans with two of his buddies to go on a camping trip for several days. They pooled their money and rented a brand-new car and bought some franks and a barbecue grill. I watched from my window as they packed the car. They were all excited and so proud of the beautiful red, air-conditioned car that was to take them on their first three-day trip to an upstate lake. At last they were ready and waved goodbye.

Once again I prayed a mother's prayer that God would keep them safe from danger and harm. I asked God to be with them every turn of the wheels and let them have a good time and bring them home safely with pleasant memories to look back on.

That evening about eleven o'clock, they were still on my mind. I prayed fervently for the Holy Spirit to protect them. About that same time, David told me later, after their long drive and a few hours at the lake, they retired to a motel and were watching television. One of the boys wanted to go out and drive around the town. He asked David to go along with him, but something seemed to tell David not to go. He pleaded with his friend to stay since it was very dark and the roads unfamiliar. He had enough for one day and was extremely tired, but his friend went anyway.

When he did not return after several hours, the others became nervous and worried. About three in the morning, a policeman brought their buddy back to the motel with his head swathed in bandages. He had been in an accident, then taken to a hospital where he was treated and released. Thank God for a miracle that he survived when the car was totaled. The passenger's side was demolished, and even the barbecue grill in the trunk was broken into little pieces.

Two hours later, they were enroute home by taxi, bus, and train, carrying all their cartons, suitcases, and guitar. They had to assist their injured buddy who was badly cut and bruised, but still able to walk. Coincidence, you say? No, but a definite answer to prayer. He is a mighty God who answers prayers in a miraculous way.

> He shall give his angels charge over thee, to keep thee in all thy ways.
>
> *Psalm 91:11*

Ask God for help in all your decisions. Ask God to help your loved ones. He loves them more than you can ever love them. Nothing is too small or too big for God. Like Solomon, who asked for wisdom and received exceeding abundance above all that he could ask or think, all these things shall be added to you too.

> Call unto me, and I will answer thee, and show thee great and mighty things, which thou knowest not.
>
> *Jeremiah 33:3*

What a powerful promise! You know, all of us are not asking to be millionaires. Wealth is not only to be thought of in terms of material or temporal possessions. To live in peace and joy and health, surrounded by loved ones and friends, is more precious than anything money can buy.

You must take God into your plans first. He will help you to attain your goals and help you to live better, richer lives. Make your life count for Him.

If you want to enrich your life, then seek first the Kingdom of God and His righteousness and all of these things shall be added unto you. These are not my words, but His very own.

For it is your Father's good pleasure to give you the kingdom.

Luke 12:32

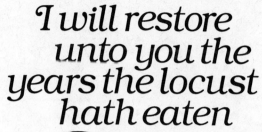

I will restore
unto you the
years the locust
hath eaten

Deciduous plants begin to wither in the fall, the leaves drop off, and all through the winter they appear lifeless. In springtime the sap begins to flow, the buds open, and the plant comes to life again.

> For, lo, the winter is past, the rain is over and gone. The flowers appear on the earth; the time of the singing of birds is come, and the voice of the turtle is heard in our land. The fig tree putteth forth her green figs, and the vines with the tender grape give a good smell.
>
> *Song of Solomon 2:11–13*

Spring seems to be one of the most beautiful seasons of the year. It brings resurrection and the promise of new life after the long, cold, and dark winter. Fresh-smelling breezes fill us with hope and anticipation for the coming days.

Now I have come to the realization that, like the deciduous plants, I have been dormant too long. The winter is over, and it is time to emerge and sing praises. By the grace of God—amazing grace beyond my wildest dreams—I have been set free to start over again and live a life more dedicated to Him. He found it a required thing to change all of my life—my home, my job, my personality, and even the new people that came into my life. These are indications of blessings being poured out.

I began to wonder what I could do for the Lord right where I live, in my small corner. I learned that it is not necessary to be a pastor, evangelist, or missionary in order to talk about Christ and to serve Him. We can all do something even though it may be on a small scale. God made each of us to be a different vessel, and He must use each vessel as He sees fit in order to fulfill the purpose for which it was created.

Paul tells us in I Corinthians 12 that God has arranged all the parts of the body just as He wanted them to be, and all the parts—the eyes, ears, arms, legs, heart, and lungs work together to make up a useful functioning body. The hands cannot say to the feet, "I don't need you." The eye cannot say to the ear, "I don't need you." In the body of Christ, all have the same Spirit, but the gifts are diversified. Some are apostles, some are prophets, some teachers, some work miracles, and some heal. We can all do something, no matter how little it seems. We can all plant "seeds."

God has a specific job for each one of us. Every Spirit-filled believer is part of the Body of Christ, and we must serve Him right where we are, whether it is working in an office, in a kitchen with pots and pans, or out in the mission field. Paul beseeched us to walk worthy of the vocation wherewith we are called. You have a definite ministry to fill a need in the very place where you are now. You are needed. You are important to God. What can you do? You can be a faith partner or a prayer partner. You can help simply by sharing, no matter how little you have to give (see Mark 12:43, 44).

There are men and women today who have received special anointing. These saints are chosen vessels unto God, called by Him to be leaders in churches, in evangelistic crusades, and in building Christian schools and cathedrals for His glory. They cannot do the work without partners, and this is where you and I fit in. Someone has to assume leadership. We cannot all be the builders, but we can all do our share by helping to support those ministries for the purpose of evangelizing the world. We cannot all go into the world as missionaries, but we can aid in the training and sending of those who can go.

> For whosoever shall call upon the name of the Lord shall be saved. How then shall they call on Him In whom they have not believed? and how shall they believe in Him of whom they have not heard? and how shall they hear without a preacher? and how shall they preach, except they be sent?
>
> *Romans 10:13–15*

Consider the television and radio ministries that come across the air waves to nearly every nation on earth. This is a very vital branch of the missionary field and one in which we can participate with very little effort. Their first concern is to go into the world preaching the Gospel to every creature, and this missionary arm reaches untold millions. They seek first the Kingdom of God and His righteousness, and their untiring efforts are rewarded when lost souls are won to Christ wherever their voices are heard. These ministries are loved and faithfully supported by their partners.

Though our part seems so small, each one of us is important. Together we can accomplish great things. Many local churches have building funds. What a great sense of accomplishment when the job is finished. No one did it alone, but every one participated in some measure, great or small. We can all enjoy the finished work, knowing that we were laborers together.

> I have planted, Apollos watered; but God gave the increase. So then neither is he that planteth any thing, neither is he that watereth; but God that giveth the increase. Now he that planteth and he that watereth are one: and every man shall receive his own reward according to his own labor.
>
> *I Corinthians 3:6–8*

Some folks are bent on fighting against God's anointed ministries and criticize when a call for financial assistance goes out. Nevertheless, these ministries survive and prosper in their great battle for the Lord despite all the fiery darts of discouragement, jealousy, and criticism aimed at them. They survive because they please God by giving Him all the glory and praise. God knows which ministries honor Him, and He will bless those that do.

> Refrain from these men, and let them alone; for if this counsel or this work be of men, it will come to nought; but if it be of God, ye cannot overthrow it; lest haply ye be found even to fight against God.
>
> *Acts 5:38–39*

You may not realize it yet, but you can literally enjoy God while you serve Him. In Sunday school we learned the catechism, "Man's chief end is to serve God and enjoy Him forever." Over and over again in Scripture we are told that if we seek Him, trust Him, and delight in Him, He will take care of our needs and we will enjoy His benefits. I slowly learned this lesson myself.

Earlier I mentioned that while I was unemployed for a time, I sought only jobs in my own neighborhood. Commuting back and forth to work three hours a day can be extremely fatiguing, and I had hoped to avoid that probability. As it turned out, I did get a job in the City requiring that much commuting time, and the job was well worth it. Several years later, however, I received an unexpected telephone call inquiring if I were still interested in filling a position that I had applied for in the past. This was truly a miraculous answer to prayer for me. Although it was a much delayed answer and for reasons I can now understand, God did grant my request. I am now working only minutes away from home in a small private school in a lovely parklike setting.

All things seemed to work together for me at this time. I was anxious to be "about my Father's business." The Holy Spirit seemed to be prompting and preparing me to go ahead and gather my thoughts about the flowers. As I began to research and compile material for the book, so many little blessings seemed to come my way. A snapshot turned up that my father had taken of me posing with my bouquet of wildflowers forty years earlier during one of our Sunday walks in the woods. Of all the family pictures ever taken, why was that the only one still around after all these years? It helped me to recall many of those walks I wrote about in Chapter 5. Friends brought me little books and articles about flowers at precisely the right time in my research. Another friend brought me a little poem he wrote, which I have included in this book. I received so many beautiful letters from strangers to whom I had written for material relating to plant life. Without a doubt, miracles were coming my way.

> I will restore to you the years that the locust hath eaten. ... And ye shall eat in plenty, and be satisfied, and praise the name of the Lord your God, that hath dealt wondrously with you.
>
> *Joel 2:25, 26*

Shall he not much more clothe you?

In Deuteronomy, chapter 8, we read how a loving, caring God led the Israelites in the wilderness and fed them with manna, which they had never seen before. For forty years they ate the food God provided and never had to worry that the supply would diminish. He saw to it that in those forty years, their clothing never got old and their shoes never wore out (see Deuteronomy 29:5, 6).

In the end, He brought them into "a good land, a land of brooks of water, of fountains and depths that spring out of valleys and hills; a land of wheat, and barley, and vines, and fig trees, and pomegranates; a land of oil olive, and honey; a land wherein thou shalt eat bread without scarceness, thou shalt not lack any thing in it" (Deuteronomy 8:7, 8).

All that He required of them was that they keep His commandments and walk in His ways.

This is the same God who takes care of us today. Trust Him.

As a single parent, I am living on much less than I had before, but I have found that God blesses the little I have, and it goes further. He sees to it that I have all I need and even some to share. Praise God, my cup runneth over!

Better is little with fear of the Lord than great wealth with turmoil.

You may earn a great deal of money, but if you have no time for God, His blessing will not be in it. You will never have enough no matter how much you get.

Whoever loves money never has money enough, whoever loves wealth is never satisfied with his income.

Ecclesiastes 5:10 NIV

Listen to what the prophet Haggai said about earnings:

Ye have sown much, and bring in little; ye eat, but ye have not enough; ye drink, but ye are not filled with drink; ye clothe you, but there is none warm; and he that earneth wages earneth wages to put it into a bag with holes.

Haggai 1:6

When the Israelites returned to Jerusalem from their Babylonian captivity under the reign of King Darius, they started building a foundation for God's Temple, but soon lost interest in the work. God warned the people through the prophet Haggai that if they continued to build fine homes for themselves while God's Temple lay in waste and ruins, their labors would produce little. He sent a drought upon the land so that nothing grew and all their efforts proved futile.

When the people obeyed the message of the Lord spoken by Haggai, their spirits were stirred up. They resumed work on the Temple, and God said,

"... Be strong ... and work. For I am with you," declares the Lord Almighty. "This is what I covenanted with you when you came out of Egypt. And my Spirit remains among you. Do not fear.... I will shake all nations, and the desired of all nations will come, and I will fill this house with glory.... The silver is mine and the gold is mine.... The glory of this present house will be greater than the glory of the former house.... And in this place I will grant peace...." From this day on I will bless you.

Haggai 2:4–9, 19 NIV

If you want God's blessing, if you want prosperity and abundant living, you can only have it if you build your life around Him. Let God be a part of your daily living, and you will grow and blossom as never before.

Are you beginning to wonder how all of this relates to the flowers? David made this comparison between man and flowers:

As for man, his days are as grass: as a flower of the field, so he flourisheth.

Psalm 103:15

Flowers that are cultivated in a garden differ from wild flowers in that they are planted, watered, fertilized, and tended by a gardener. You are like a lovely flower growing in God's garden. You are intricately designed, fragile, and beautiful, yet you are more hardy and adaptable to extreme conditions than you realize. In order to grow, He sends the rain as well as the sun upon you. The flower needs both if it is to thrive.

Take heart, dear one. God loves you very much. He made you a beautiful being. You are someone special, capable of contributing to the well-being of others. He put you where you are because someone where you live or where you work needs what only you can offer. Find out what your purpose is in your little place under the sun, for someone is depending on you for love and care.

Face life with a new outlook. Look around and begin to appreciate all the beauty God has given you to enjoy. Come out of the shadows and into the sunshine of His love. Walk along a beach and listen to the waves lapping on the shore and hear the cry of the gulls. See the sunshine sparkling and glistening on the dancing waves, the way a diamond catches the light's rays, sending spectroscopes of dazzling colors bouncing off the walls. Walk in the park where there are flowers and fountains. Try to sketch the scene in your memory so that it can be remembered again at some future time. "I gazed—and gazed, but little thought, what wealth the show to me had brought," said Wordsworth,[33] recalling the vision of a field of flowers he had once seen. Radiate joy and happiness to others, and you will find it to be quite contagious.

May your presence be like one of the lovely blossoms bringing joy to the beholder. You, little flower, have some honey in the making. Soon there will be someone coming around to collect it. Will you be able to sweeten the life of your friend, your neighbor, or even a stranger?

Let God take care of you as you grow and mature. Keep your face lifted toward the Son. Welcome the showers as well as the sunshine. Trust Him, for the Gardener knows how much of each to send your way. Then you will bloom and flourish to bring beauty and fragrance into the lives of others.

The next time you visit a flower show or garden, take a closer look at the blossoms. Look into the upturned face of each beautiful flower and let your thoughts dwell on them. You will find no trace of anxiety, only a sense of well-being, satisfaction, and contentment, along with exquisite beauty. The fragrant flowers with velvet-soft petals are perfection—an expression of God's creativity, an extension of His great love.

God, who clothes the flowers regally without need for anxious labor on their part, will clothe and feed you if you make Him your first desire. Never again will a flower be just a pretty ornament to you, but it will be a silent reminder to consider the lilies ... and to

Take no thought, saying, What shall we eat? or, What shall we drink? or, Wherewithal shall we be clothed?

Matthew 6:31

If God so clothe the grass of the field, which today is, and tomorrow is cast into the oven, shall he not much more clothe you, O ye of little faith?

Matthew 6:30

156

I am the Rose of Sharon, and the Lily of the Valleys.

Song of Solomon 2:1

Praise the Lord! Amen.

Afterword

E ver since I started working on this book, I have been a frequent visitor of local libraries, borrowing books pertaining to the plant world. Of course I chose books that were elementary in nature, rather than those with very technical phraseology. That meant I had to look in the Children's Section, where many delightful books on botany can be found.

After acquiring a basic knowledge of the world of flowers, I was ready to go out with my wildflower guide and camera to collect and scrutinize some real live specimens. The very simple research I embarked on has triggered in me a desire to learn so much more about the botanical world. It is a fascinating field, filled with strange and wonderful inhabitants.

I do not pretend to know a great deal about plant life, but I only wish to focus your thoughts on the higher power and wisdom behind each tiny plant. You will find a loving, caring God, who gave so much attention and minute detail to every creation in the universe.

Jesus was never too busy to notice the lilies of the field, the fig tree, the mustard seeds, the grape vine, and the wheat fields. When He walked and talked with His disciples, He paid attention to many of the little things around Him. He based many of His sermons and parables on these. He spoke of the sparrows that neither sowed nor reaped, the tiny mustard seed growing into a great tree, the tares growing among the wheat and the fruitless branches that must be removed from the vine.

One of my favorite summer pastimes is walking wherever there are flowers and trees. To my delight, summer walks in local parks uncovered some of the loveliest flowering weeds, which I had barely noticed before. My son accompanied me on one of these walks and appeared quite bored. He probably wondered if his mother was perhaps overdoing this "romping-in-the-woods-like-a-kid" bit. In order not to miss anything, I asked him to observe the left side of the road while I observed the right. At first he seemed reluctant, but he soon got caught up in the mood of our activity when he spotted a cluster of bright orange flowers on top of a steep hill. He pointed them out and asked if I would like to have them. Since the hill was too steep for me to climb, he, being a good sport, offered to go up to get them. Rather than disturb the flowers, which were bright orange day lilies, I gave him the camera to take several pictures. Unfortunately, he was wearing shorts and sandals that day. When he returned, his legs from the knees down were scratched and bleeding from the thorny brush he waded through. While dodging a bee, he almost missed getting the day lilies in the picture.

On the same afternoon, which was an extremely hot day, we photographed Queen Anne's lace, yarrow, chicory, butter-and-eggs, thistles, Saint Johnsworts, vetches, day lilies, water lilies, and cattails. You have probably seen all of these wildflowers many times. I am not yet familiar with a great many of the plants I find, but I hope to learn about them eventually.

Being somewhat of a collector of "things" like stamps, old bottles, and other nostalgic memorabilia, I have recently stumbled onto a new, engrossing pastime—that of collecting, cutting, and pressing flowers. For the nature lover, this can be an inexpensive hobby and a most rewarding one. It costs very little to pluck a weed or pick up a brightly colored fallen leaf, press it between newspaper pages under some heavy books, and wait a few weeks. After pressing, arrange them on a plastic place mat, plain box, or container. Then cover them with clear contact paper. You can probably find many interesting ideas in magazines, or you can invent your own originals. Keep in mind that many rare wildflowers are rapidly becoming endangered species. They are best left undisturbed in their natural habitat.

As I began to learn the unusual names of some of the more common weeds growing in my neighborhood parks and lots, my curiosity was aroused as to the source of some of their quaint names. Many plants have nicknames that originate from the appearance of the flowers or leaves. One look and you could almost name them yourself. For instance, it's very obvious why the "omnipresent" Queen Anne's lace received its name. The large, flat cluster of white flowers looks like a lace doily. Most of them have one tiny purple floret in the center. From books I learned that this plant is also known as the *wild carrot* because it has a long carrot-shaped root. And so it does, I pulled one up to see for myself. When the flower turns brown and begins to seed, it curls up into a hollow ball resembling a bird's nest; thus, it is also given the name *bird's nest plant*. Still another name given to it by farmers is *devil's plague*, probably because it spreads abundantly everywhere. One more interesting thought on this weed that populates every field and roadside is the fact that insects love its large landing field. The nectar is easily accessible to almost every kind of insect. In contrast, another flower is called *monkshood* because its hood or helmet shape can only be pollinated by one insect—the bumblebee. The bee is especially equipped with proboscises long enough to reach nectar deeply embedded in the folded petals. As the bee reaches in to collect the nectar, the stamen of the flower, which has a brush-like "attachment" on the end, reaches down to rub pollen on the bee's back.

My favorite name is kiss-me-over-the-garden-gate, also known as *Johnny-jump-up*. This wild pansy probably got its name because it springs up rather quickly.

Other descriptive names are jack-in-the-pulpit, bleeding heart, bluebells, Dutchman's breeches, Indian pipe (an all white plant containing no chlorophyll), and monkey flower, which has markings resembling a grinning monkey face. The jewelweed, named because the flowers look like dainty hanging earrings, is also called *touch-me-not* or *quick-in-the-hand* because its seed pods break open at the slightest touch and the seeds shoot out. Butter-and-eggs gets its amusing name from its attractive yellow-orange color; it is also called *snapdragon.* If you squeeze the flower, the mouth opens wide.

There is an element of surprise and wonder in every species. What marvelous combinations of color and texture and what uniqueness of design to be found in plants.

Many weeds are named according to the appearance of their leaves. The venus's-flytrap has leaves that characterize jaws, and the leaves do just what the name suggests. Arrowheads growing in marshes and near water bear leaves shaped like arrowheads. Its potato-like tubers are eaten by ducks. Indians also ate the duck potatoes they gathered from the water.

Another marsh plant is the cattail, a tall reed topped with a fuzzy brown spike-like flower that supposedly resembles the tail of a frightened cat. If you want to collect these plants to decorate your home, be sure to let them dry out first in your garage. The flowers have been known to explode in the warmth of the home and the spores make an awful mess. Indians used the down for stuffing mattresses.

Cinquefoil or five-fingers has five-lobed leaflets shaped like fingers. Goosefoot has large leaves shaped like the feet of a goose. Cockleburs or sticktights are unusual names, but when the brown prickly seeds stick to your clothing, you will not forget their names. The familiar morning glories, four-o'clocks, and moonflowers all bloom at the time their names indicate. The night-blooming cereus is a beautiful cactus flower that opens at night. The dayflower is another common weed with blue blossoms that open for a few hours on warm, bright days.

One fascinating discovery after another prompted me to seek more information on the many ways seeds travel. Some seeds are shot like missiles from their parent plant. Some creep along the ground on long spines that open and close (the sneezeweed is one). Some seeds are transported by ants. The beggar's-ticks, cockleburs, and sandburs stick with barbed spines to animals and clothing. Seeds from the dandelion and silkweed sail through the air on downy parachutes. Wild geranium and jewelweed project seeds like a slingshot. The tumbleweed rolls around, planting its own seeds. Seeds of the maple tree are borne through the air on "wings," which carry them some distance away. Some seeds are coated with sticky substances, causing them to adhere to birds and animals until wiped off. Whatever means the parent plant employs, all the seeds are carried in some unusual manner far enough away so that they will have room to grow. However, not every dispersed seed lives to fruition. The chances of the giant saguaro seeds reaching maturity and bearing fruit are 40 million to one. Chances of the giant sequoia seeds, which are the size of a pinhead, growing to maturity are 1 billion to one.

Some very unusual plants worthy of mention are the obedient plant, whose flowers swivel on joints, so that at a touch of the finger you can make the blossoms move around. The telegraph plant has two tiny leaflets at the base of each large leaf. These two leaflets flutter up and down like a telegraph signal. The prayer plant has leaves that move too. In keeping with its name, the leaves fold up at night almost as though they were praying. Often while eating breakfast in my kitchen, I hear the leaves brushing against each other as they open for the day.

I have only mentioned some of the unusual trappings and charming names, but there are thousands of interesting facts about plants that you can read about in your library or see at your local nursery. Hopefully, these thoughts on flowers will ignite your curiosity into the exciting world of nature's greenery. This is indeed captivating, inspiring material for thought; a subject which anyone at any age can pursue with genuine pleasure.

Plants, like people, struggle to survive in their little patch of ground among many rivals. From the moment the seed sprouts, its stem reaches and twists toward the sun as it grows, blossoms, bears fruit, and drops seed.

There can be little doubt that the plant world, with all its intricate mechanisms and timing devices, could have only been designed by a divine Creator.

There are so many other kinds of miracles taking place in our lives and in our world every day. What enables a dog to pick up a person's scent and track this invisible trail for many miles? What instinct causes geese and ducks to migrate at a particular time, and why do they fly in a V-formation enroute? Why do birds navigate thousands of miles along the same course as their predecessors and converge along the same valleys and mountain ranges to feed and rest? Why do salmon make the exhausting swim upstream, only to spawn in the same fresh water spot as their ancestors? By instinct they know when the time comes to begin their difficult migration.

Who gives intuition and instinct?

Job 38:36 LB

The next time you visit your library, read the amazing story of the night-spawning grunions. Not only do they arrive on the Southern California coast on a predictable night, but they hit the beach soon after the peak of high tide, dig two-inch holes in the sand, the females deposit about 2,000 eggs each, the males fertilize the eggs, and the parent fish return to sea on the ebb of the very next wave, all in a period of 25 seconds—faster than it took me to write this. Two weeks later, at high tide, the baby grunions have hatched and are returned to the sea by the waves. All of this action must be precisely regulated to coincide with the tides.

Who decreed the boundaries of the seas ... and said "Thus far and no farther shall you come, and here shall your proud waves stop!"?

Job 38:8–11 LB

Perhaps you will get a probable scientific explanation for these amazing phenomena from a book, but the bottom line is that these are all miracles from God. You will find a thrilling account of the wisdom of God, who governs all nature and the universe, in Job 36:22 through chapter 41.

The entire ecosystem is a complex, awesome plan bigger than the human mind can fathom. Like a series of mighty miracles, it encompasses the growth of a large plant from a very tiny seed, the reproductive process involving insects of every kind, the production of nectar and honey to feed the birds and insects and fruit and vegetables to feed man and animals, and the scattering of seeds year after year, century after century. Everything grows, withers, dies, and repeats the cycle the next generation, performing the purpose which God intended. The insects depend on the plants to sustain them, and the plants depend on the insects to fertilize them and, in some cases, to disperse the seeds for their regeneration.

> Oh Lord, how manifold are thy works! In wisdom hast thou made them all: the earth is full of thy riches.
>
> *Psalm 104:24*

Since you are more precious to Him than the flowers of the field, be assured that He has a plan and purpose for your life. You are a wonderful, marvelous creation, intricately designed and unique from all the rest. Learn to trust your Creator and never cease to praise Him for His wonderful works.

Notes

1. Reverend Charles H. Spurgeon, *Spurgeon's Gems Being Brilliant Passages from the Discourses of the Rev. C. H. Spurgeon* (Old Tappan, N.J.: Fleming H. Revell Company), p. 175.

2. Dr. Robert H. Schuller is pastor and founder of the Garden Grove Community Church in Garden Grove, Ca., and is seen weekly on the internationally acclaimed television program, "Hour of Power."

3. The tulip is the Netherlands' national symbol; the lily, Italy's; and the thistle, Scotland's.

4. W.R. Goodman, "Desert Sand," *Sunshine and Shadows* (New Rochelle, N.Y.: Salesian Missions of Saint John Bosco, 1982). All rights reserved.

5. Henry D. Thoreau in Mary W. Tileston, *Daily Strength for Daily Needs* (New York: Grosset & Dunlap, Inc., by arrangement with Little, Brown and Company, 1928), p. 170.

6. Alfred, Lord Tennyson, "Flower in the Crannied Wall," *Bartlett's Familiar Quotations*, 14th ed. (Boston: Little, Brown and Company, 1968), p. 654B.

7. Archbishop Francois Fenelon, *Let Go.* Copyright © 1973 by Banner Publishing/Whitaker House, Pittsburgh & Colfax Streets, Springdale, Pa. 15144, letter 15, p. 30.

8. Jane Crewdson in Tileston, *Daily Strength for Daily Needs*, p. 74.

9. Saint Francis de Sales in Tileston, *Daily Strength for Daily Needs*, p. 29.

10. Ralph Waldo Emerson in Frank Mead, *Encyclopedia of Religious Quotations* (Old Tappan, N.J.: Fleming H. Revell Company, 1965), p. 132.

11. William Wordsworth, "I Wandered Lonely as a Cloud," *The Complete Poetical Works of William Wordsworth* (New York: Macmillan Publishing Co., Inc., 1930), p. 205.

12. Ibid., p. 205.

13. William Shakespeare, *Romeo and Juliet* (act II, scene II), from *Four Great Tragedies by William Shakespeare* (New York: Washington Square Press, Inc., 1948), p. 43, lines 11 and 12.

14. Amy Lowell, "Lilacs" from *The Complete Poetical Works of Amy Lowell* (Boston: Houghton Mifflin Company, 1955), p. 446. Copyright 1955 by Houghton Mifflin Company. Reprinted by permission of Houghton Mifflin Company.

15. From "Birches" from *The Poetry of Robert Frost* edited by Edward Connery Lathem. Copyright 1916, © 1969 Holt, Rinehart and Winston. Copyright 1944 by Robert Frost. Reprinted by permission of Holt, Rinehart and Winston, Publishers.

16. Sister Miriam Gallagher (1886–1966), "The Root of Jesse," *Woven of the Sky* (Religious Sisters of Mercy of the Union, Scranton Province, Dallas, Pa.).

17. Spurgeon, *Spurgeon's Gems*, p. 11.

18. Anonymous, "Only One Life," in *Our Daily Bread* (Grand Rapids, Mi.: Radio Bible Class), vol. 27, no. 10, January 25, 1983.

19. Spurgeon, *Spurgeon's Gems*, p. 175.

20. William Shakespeare, "Sonnet XV", from *The Pocket Book of Verse*, edited by M.E. Speare (New York: Washington Square Press, Inc., 1940), p. 12.

21. Anonymous, "What, Giving Again?" in *Our Daily Bread*, n.d.

22. Reverend William A. Parsons, Park Street United Methodist Church, Troy, Ala. Letter used by permission.

23. John Donne, "No Man Is an Island," in Frank Mead, *Encyclopedia of Religious Quotations* (Old Tappan, N.J.: Fleming H. Revell Company, 1965), p. 100.

24. Anonymous, "Friends," in *Our Daily Bread*, vol. 21, no. 5, August 1, 1976.

25. The following books are written about or by "overcomers": Joni Eareckson with Joe Musser, *Joni* (Grand Rapids, Mi.: Zondervan

Publishing House, 1976); Max Cleland, *Strong at the Broken Places* (Lincoln, Va.: Chosen Books, 1980); Diane Bringgold, *Life Instead* (Waco, Tx.: Word, Inc., 1979); Merrill Womack and Virginia Womack with Mel White and Lyla White, *Tested by Fire* (Old Tappan, N.J.: Fleming H. Revell Company, 1976); George Otis with Norman Williams, *Terror at Tenerife* (Van Nuys, Ca.: Bible Voice, Inc., 1977).

26. Robert Browning, "Rabbi Ben Ezra," *Bartlett's Familiar Quotations*, 14th ed. (Boston: Little, Brown and Company, 1968), p. 666A.

27. Steven Marc Bernstein, "Flowers." Poem used by permission.

28. Henry van Dyke, "A Handful of Clay," in *The Blue Flower* (New York: Charles Scribner's Sons, 1902), pp. 199–205.

29. Reverend Oral Roberts is president and founder of Oral Roberts University in Tulsa, Ok. His weekly television show is called *Oral Roberts and You.*

30. Alice Hansche Mortenson, "I Needed the Quiet," *I Needed the Quiet* (Kansas City, Mo.: Beacon Hill Press, 1978). Used by permission.

31. William Newton Clark in Frank Mead, *Encyclopedia of Religious Quotations* (Old Tappan, N.J.: Fleming H. Revell Company, 1965), p. 131.

32. Saint Francis of Assisi, *The Perfect Joy of St. Francis*, ed. by Felix Timmermans, trans. Raphael Brown (New York: Farrar, Straus & Giroux, Inc., 1955), p. 82.

33. William Wordsworth, "I Wandered Lonely as a Cloud," in *The Complete Poetical Works of William Wordsworth* (New York: Macmillan Publishing Co., Inc. 1930), p. 205.

The information used in Chapter 10, "Beauty from Ashes," was furnished on request, and I wish to express grateful appreciation for the courtesies extended by the following:

City of Los Angeles Department of Fire, Public Service Unit, 200 North Main Street, Los Angeles, Ca. 90012, for material on the Los Angeles Hills brush conflagration, November 1961.

Peshtigo Times, West Front Street, Peshtigo, Wi. 54157, for information on the historical Peshtigo fire of October 8, 1871.

Darrell A. Posey, "The Keepers of the Forest," from *Garden* magazine of The New York Botanical Garden (January/February),

© 1982, p. 18, for excerpt on slash and burn farming technique in the Amazon forest.

Arizona-Sonora Desert Museum, Route 9, Box 900, Tucson, Az. 85704, for facts on cacti and birds of the desert.

U.S. Department of Agriculture, Forest Service, Press Officer, P.O. Box 2417, Washington, D.C. 20013, for furnishing information on fire's effects on chaparral, fireweed, and other plants.